Beyond Cost-per-Unit

Economic Analysis and Metrics in Defense Decisionmaking

KATHARINA LEY BEST, VICTORIA A. GREENFIELD, CRAIG A. BOND,
NATHANIEL EDENFIELD, MARK HVIZDA, JOHN C. JACKSON,
DUNCAN LONG, JORDAN WILLCOX

Prepared for or the United States Army
Approved for public release; distribution is unlimited.

For more information on this publication, visit **www.rand.org/t/RRA1802-2**.

About RAND

The RAND Corporation is a research organization that develops solutions to public policy challenges to help make communities throughout the world safer and more secure, healthier and more prosperous. RAND is nonprofit, nonpartisan, and committed to the public interest. To learn more about RAND, visit www.rand.org.

Research Integrity

Our mission to help improve policy and decisionmaking through research and analysis is enabled through our core values of quality and objectivity and our unwavering commitment to the highest level of integrity and ethical behavior. To help ensure our research and analysis are rigorous, objective, and nonpartisan, we subject our research publications to a robust and exacting quality-assurance process; avoid both the appearance and reality of financial and other conflicts of interest through staff training, project screening, and a policy of mandatory disclosure; and pursue transparency in our research engagements through our commitment to the open publication of our research findings and recommendations, disclosure of the source of funding of published research, and policies to ensure intellectual independence. For more information, visit www.rand.org/about/research-integrity.

RAND's publications do not necessarily reflect the opinions of its research clients and sponsors.

About This Report

This report documents research and analysis conducted as part of a project entitled *Army Cost-per-Effect Analysis*, sponsored by the Deputy Chief of Staff, G-3/5/7, U.S. Army. The purpose of the project was to assess the feasibility and utility of a cost-per-effect metric to complement existing qualitative and quantitative assessments and comparisons of cost versus benefit in planned systems and capabilities development for the Army and other armed services.

This research was conducted within RAND Arroyo Center's Strategy, Doctrine, and Resources Program. RAND Arroyo Center, part of the RAND Corporation, is a federally funded research and development center (FFRDC) sponsored by the United States Army.

RAND operates under a "Federal-Wide Assurance" (FWA00003425) and complies with the *Code of Federal Regulations for the Protection of Human Subjects Under United States Law* (45 CFR 46), also known as "the Common Rule," as well as with the implementation guidance set forth in DoD Instruction 3216.02. As applicable, this compliance includes reviews and approvals by RAND's Institutional Review Board (the Human Subjects Protection Committee) and by the U.S. Army. The views of sources used in this study are solely their own and do not represent the official policy or position of DoD or the U.S. Government.

Acknowledgments

We are extremely grateful for the support we received from our study sponsors within G-3/5/7. We would especially like to thank COL J. P. Clark, LTC Ryan McCarthy, and MAJ Nick Morton, who helped us identify needed contacts and data, and COL David Spencer, who helped us see this project through to its conclusion. Additionally, thanks to Megan Malone, Pranaz Ciziunas, and Jack Zeto for providing needed information for development of examples. We are thankful for the support of RAND colleagues Henry Hargrove, Barry Wilson, and Steve Seabrook in developing and vetting model inputs; Christopher Mouton in sharing related work and insights; and Emily Haglund, Francisco Walter, and Lily Hoak in finalizing this report. Thanks also to RAND Army Fellow MAJ Eliot Proctor for his assistance. Finally, we would like to thank our reviewers, Elizabeth Hastings Roer and Jennifer Lamping Lewis, and the leadership in the Arroyo Center's Strategy, Doctrine, and Resources Program, Molly Dunigan and Jon Wong. Any remaining errors are our own.

Summary

The research reported here was completed in May 2023, followed by security review by the sponsor and the U.S. Army Office of the Chief of Public Affairs, with final sign-off in May 2024.

In July 2020, the Mitchell Institute for Aerospace Studies (the Mitchell Institute) published a report entitled *Resolving America's Defense Strategy-Resource Mismatch: The Case for Cost-per-Effect Analysis.*[1] The thesis of this report is that the U.S. Air Force—and the Department of Defense (DoD) at large—should prioritize weapon systems that "yield maximum mission value" rather than "rely on overly simplistic metrics," such as per-unit acquisitions costs or cost-per-flying-hour, that do not account for differences in capabilities across systems for decisionmaking.[2] The authors' recommended approach is a metric that they call "cost-per-effect," or CPE. The proposed CPE metric "measures the sum of what it takes to net a desired mission result, not just a single system's acquisition and support costs without necessary context surrounding the capability's actual use" and is a form of cost-effectiveness analysis (CEA).[3]

Against this backdrop, the U.S. Army G-3/5/7 asked RAND Arroyo Center to assess the feasibility and utility of a CPE metric as a complement to existing approaches to assessing costs and benefits in planned systems and capabilities development for the Army and other armed services. To conduct this assessment, we first reviewed the small literature on CPE analysis and the larger literature on related forms of economic analysis, including CEA, that are used to support decisionmaking. Using the literature, we developed a theoretical framework for economic analysis that assesses cost effectiveness and yields a CPE-like metric. Then, in consultation with the sponsor, we selected a notional battlefield scenario with which we could explore an application of economic analysis—specifically, CEA—by comparing the costs of several technology options for achieving a desired outcome. We applied the framework to the notional example qualitatively and drew additional insight from sample calculations that explored the effects of variation in the battlefield context, the presence of benefits and costs beyond the objective, the need to consider multiple objectives, and the inclusion and exclusion of various cost categories. Although we exclude the sample calculations from this report for sensitivity reasons, we present the theoretical framework, the qualitative application, and related insights for economic analysis in defense decisionmaking.

---

[1] David A. Deptula and Douglas A. Birkey, *Resolving America's Defense Strategy-Resource Mismatch: The Case for Cost-per-Effect Analysis*, Mitchell Institute for Aerospace Studies, July 2020.

[2] Deptula and Birkey, 2020, p. 1.

[3] Deptula and Birkey, 2020, p. 1.

We proceed by offering a brief introduction to different types of economic analysis and laying out the set of considerations related to the difficulty of performing economic analysis. We then revisit these considerations in light of the battlefield-level example.

Types of Economic Analysis

Department of Defense Instruction (DoDI) 7041.03 defines *economic analysis* as "[a] systematic approach to the problem of choosing the best method of allocating scarce resources to achieve a given *objective*" (emphasis added) and "includes consideration of costs, benefits, risk, and uncertainty."[4] The terms of the DoDI apply to a broad variety of resource allocation decisions, including those involving "startup research, acquisition, renewal, renovation, conversion, upgrade, expansion, pre-planned product improvement, leasing, or operations of all programs or projects." DoDI 7041.03, Army guidance,[5] and other federal guidance point to CEA, cost-benefit analysis (CBA), and business case analysis (BCA) as different methods for conducting economic analyses, which suggests treating *economic analysis* as an umbrella term.

In a CBA, both the costs and the benefits of meeting an objective are monetized as much as possible, which enables the derivation of a *net benefit* (the monetary value of the benefits minus the monetary value of the costs, for any means of meeting an objective).[6] The net benefit, typically evaluated as a *net present value*, constitutes the primary *metric* associated with CBA. Net benefit calculations can be used to decide whether a weapon system, program, strategy, or tactic is *worth it* (i.e., whether the benefits outweigh the costs) and to compare not only different paths for pursuing the same objectives but also different paths leading to different, potentially disparate, objectives.

By comparison, in a CEA, the costs are represented monetarily, but the benefits are represented in other units or qualitatively simply as the attainment of a particular effect or objective,[7] such as disabling an adversary or prevailing in battle. A CEA can generate a metric

---

[4] DoD, *Economic Analysis for Decision-Making*, Department of Defense Instruction 7041.03, September 9, 2015, incorporating change 1, October 2, 2017, p. 18.

[5] Department of the Army Pamphlet 415-3 similarly defines economic analysis in the context of construction projects as a "structured method to identify, analyze, and compare costs and benefits of the alternatives" (Headquarters, Department of the Army, *Economic Analysis: Description and Methods*, Department of the Army Pamphlet 415-3, September 28, 2018, p. 4). The pamphlet specifies the first step in the analytical process as establishing a project objective: "The project objective is a problem statement, which defines the need the Government is attempting to answer. The reason for undertaking an EA [economic analysis] is to discern the most beneficial means of achieving a solution to a perceived problem. The project objective must be an unbiased statement of the problem, or project need" (Headquarters, Department of the Army, 2018, p. 6).

[6] See, for example, Office of Management and Budget (OMB), *Regulatory Analysis*, Circular A-4, September 17, 2003.

[7] See, for example, OMB, 2003.

consisting of a ratio, such as a CPE or cost-per-objective (CPO), which is expressed in terms of dollars per unit of the effect or objective, respectively.[8] These metrics can be used to support comparisons of the costs of alternatives for pursuing the same effect or objective (such as disabling an adversary), but they cannot tell us whether an alternative is worth it or be used to compare alternatives that are intended to yield disparate results.

BCA, by contrast, has been defined as "a decision support tool that projects the likely financial results and other business consequences of an action" and might take a more "enterprise wide" or "holistic" view of the effects of the action than a CBA or CEA.[9]

By implicitly or explicitly incorporating benefits in addition to costs, all three methods (CBA, CEA, and BCA) go beyond cost-per-unit (CPU) or looking simply at a weapon system's price tag. In our articulation of these forms of economic analysis, which stipulates an objective,[10] the main distinction between CBA and CEA lies in the extent of monetization, which has substantial implications for interpretation and utility. BCA stands somewhat apart as a tool—or toolkit—that can include or build on elements of each of the other methods. However, regardless of the method—be it a CBA, CEA, or BCA—the analyst would still need to consider the potential for *ancillary benefits* and *unintended consequences* (i.e., additional good or bad results, such as less attrition or more casualties, that are not part of the objective) and for any *risks* or *uncertainties* associated with the problem.[11] Table S.1 summarizes our comparison of these methods.

Generalizing Economic Analysis

Conducting an economic analysis, including a CEA, and deriving related metrics becomes more difficult when we face more complexity or try to insert greater realism into our analysis. Whereas *complexity* refers to the intricacy of the real-world problem (including the objective), *realism* refers to what we choose to capture in our analytic representation of the real-world

---

[8] In some cases, many of which we explore in this report, a problem can be reduced to *cost minimization* (i.e., choosing the least costly means of obtaining an outcome).

[9] Marty J. Schmidt, *The Business Case Guide*, 2nd ed., Solution Matrix, 2002, p. 1. For a more recent version of this guide, see Business Case Website, homepage, undated. The *DoD Product Support Business Case Analysis Guidebook* does not draw a sharp distinction between BCA and other forms of economic analysis but rather seems to equate them by saying that "[o]ther names for a BCA are Economic Analysis, Cost-Benefit Analysis, and Benefit-Cost Analysis." However, the guidebook also suggests that a BCA might encompass more "enterprise wide" and "holistic" concerns than other such decision support tools. See Office of the Assistant Secretary of Defense for Logistics and Materiel Readiness, *DoD Product Support Business Case Analysis Guidebook*, U.S. Department of Defense, 2014, p. 5.

[10] DoD, 2017.

[11] OMB (2003) refers to "ancillary benefits," on the one hand, and interchangeably, "undesirable side effects," "countervailing risks," and "adverse consequence," on the other hand, but the literature often uses the term "unintended consequences" to refer to the latter, even if it can include the former. Thus, whereas unintended consequences could be positive or negative, we use the term to refer to only negative consequences.

TABLE S.1

Comparison of Methods of Economic Analysis

Characteristic	CBA	CEA	BCA
Techniques	• Evaluate monetary costs, monetary benefits, ancillary benefits, unintended consequences, and risks of investment, tactics, strategy, programs, etc. that can meet objective(s)	• Evaluate monetary costs, ancillary benefits, unintended consequences, and risks of meeting objective(s) through investment, tactics, strategy, programs, etc.	• Various techniques (e.g., CBA, CEA, break-even analysis, and financial analysis)
Metrics (units)	• Net benefits (monetary *level*) are the results of the analysis • Mean, variance, CPU (monetary *ratio*) can inform the analysis	• CPE, CPO (monetary *ratio*) are the results of the analysis • Mean, variance, CPU (monetary *ratio*) can inform the analysis	• Various metrics (e.g., net benefits, CPE, CPO, CPU, ROI) can emerge from or inform the analysis
Decision rules	• Net benefits > 0 • Choose alternative with the most net benefit (maximum), subject to ancillary benefits, unintended consequences, risks, uncertainties, and other factors	• Choose alternative with the least cost (minimum), subject to ancillary benefits, unintended consequences, risks, uncertainties, and other factors	• Differ by technique(s)
Uses	• Establishing *admissibility* (Is it worth it?) and *preferability* (Is it better?) • Comparing alternatives for addressing the same or disparate objectives	• Establishing preferability but not admissibility • Comparing alternatives for addressing the same objective	• Differ by technique(s)
Information needs	• Costs, benefits • Monetary values of costs and benefits	• Costs, benefits • Monetary value of costs, but not of benefits	• Differ by technique(s)

NOTE: In cases that fall between these depictions of CBA and CEA, it might be possible to partially monetize benefits. ROI = return on investment.

problem. When we increase or decrease the realism of our analysis, we are not changing the *problem space*—which we define as the attributes or features of the real-world problem—but rather are changing how we depict it or with how much fidelity. However, although complexity and realism are distinct concepts, they are related because the greater the complexity of the problem space, the harder it can be to portray the problem space realistically.

Complexity

In the list below, we set out a typology of potential sources of complexity. Despite our seemingly clean parsing, we acknowledge that the sources of complexity are sometimes interconnected and reinforcing. For example, the level of analysis—be it an engagement, the battlefield, or a campaign—at which we specify the objective can be a source of complexity, but it can also serve as a driver of other sources of complexity. For example, as we move from engagement to battlefield to campaign, we might find it harder to pin down a single *fixed* (i.e., known, bounded, and unchanging) and measurable objective, and we might face greater risk or uncertainty in the operating environment.[12] Regardless of the level of analysis, technology, itself, can also present challenges, as when multiple weapon systems must be used together, when one weapon system can achieve more than one objective, or when we know more about one weapon system than another. For example, one technology might be well-established and battlefield-proven, a second technology might be fully developed but not battlefield-proven, and a third technology might still be under development. Different approaches to meeting an objective can also entail different ancillary benefits or unintended consequences.

Sources of complexity for an economic analysis can include

- specification of objectives
  - number of objectives
    - level(s) of objectives (i.e., engagement, battlefield, or campaign)
    - potential for sequential or nested objectives (meaning that one objective must precede another or that multiple objectives contribute to another)
    - weighting or combining objectives
  - fixity of objectives
  - constraints on attaining objectives
- relevance of ancillary benefits or unintended consequences
- nature of technology that produces effects, such as
  - a weapon system that might be able to support more than one objective
  - a weapon system that might depend on support from or cooperation with others
  - different features of a weapon system that hold different values in different use cases
- types of contexts under consideration
  - behavioral (e.g., strategic or nonstrategic) characteristics
  - nonbehavioral (e.g., temporal [single- or multi-period], physical, spatial, or other environmental) characteristics
- designation of boundaries on costs, effects, and other phenomena
  - drawing a circle around the problem space
  - defining effects and contributions to effects
- risks or uncertainties with respect to any or all of the above.

---

[12] An objective is bounded if it has clear, accepted limits (see Appendix A).

Although interconnectedness among different sources of complexity makes it hard to single out one source as more important than the rest, the extent to which an objective is known, bounded, and unchanging—which we refer to as *fixity*—stands paramount among them, along with the potential for risk and uncertainty that can undermine fixity and interact with other sources of complexity.

Realism

Producing a realistic analysis means depicting the problem space as it is, with whatever complexity it entails, at whatever level it occurs. For example, if our level of analysis is an engagement, we could add realism to our portrayal by depicting not just target location error but also target movement and defenses. Producing a realistic representation of the problem space, however, can be difficult for reasons related to technical model development and to the need for assumptions and professional judgment. Furthermore, producing a realistic representation could increase the difficulty of applying the model to perform an analysis by increasing the need for computing power and data. Costing could also become more difficult because, with more realism, we might need to break out more types of costs and be more precise about them. The challenges of adding realism would likely increase with the complexity of the problem space, but, for any given problem space, adding realism can make the exercise more difficult and might involve more fully acknowledging complexity.

Applying Cost-Effectiveness Analysis to a Distance Strike Mission

To make the theoretical discussion more concrete, we explore using a CEA in a notional example—i.e., for selecting among technologies for achieving a distance strike against an enemy target—and consider potential analytical challenges.[13]

In this notional example, we present a choice between three possible friendly (Blue) technologies that could achieve the strike objective but that each rely either more or less heavily on air- or ground-based assets. The technologies consist of activities that together produce specific effects. The Blue shooters fire at a predefined number of enemy (Red) targets to destroy them. The set of cumulative effects achieved by a technology is then measured against a desired objective to determine whether the overall strike mission has been achieved. We designed the three technologies in our example to consider various levels of inclusion of ground-based fires—in addition to a default option of air-launched fires—for this strike.

---

[13] Additional detail on this example is available in a companion report (Katharina Ley Best, Victoria A. Greenfield, Craig A. Bond, Nathaniel Edenfield, Mark Hvizda, John C. Jackson, Duncan Long, Jordan Willcox, *Beyond Cost-per-Shot: Illustrating the Use of Economic Analysis and Metrics in Defense Decisionmaking*, 2023, Not available to the general public). This section does not include results based on those details or related simulation modeling.

The technologies consist of two bookend technologies that rely most and least heavily on air-based assets compared with land-based assets and a representative, middling technology. The costs of achieving the objective, measured in dollars, differ by technology because of the differences in the asset mix.

With the strike example, we present an application of CEA to a specific technology choice and show how some of the theoretical challenges captured above can arise, even in a setting with limited complexity and realism. To illustrate just one potential source of complexity that could make the economic analysis more difficult, the strike-related objective might not be well bounded if, for example, executing the mission uncovers new threats, requiring additional resources, which in turn uncover new threats, and so on.

Still, we can translate the theoretical framing to other technology applications. To do so would require, as it does in our strike application, defining the framing features and attributes of the problem space to contain the alternative technologies, the objective, the effects, the costs, the ancillary benefits, the unintended consequences, and any sources of risk and uncertainty for the analysis. Computing and then usefully applying CEA and deriving a CPO metric to answer the question about the technology choice would then also require grappling with the set of analytic challenges, such as data availability and computational demand, laid out above. Although the basic approach would be the same in other applications, we might expect to see substantial difference across the applications, not just in the specification of the technology or the objective but also in the cost estimation, because the cost drivers and the relative order of magnitude of different cost components might be very different.

Table S.2 highlights the needed framing features and the specification requirements and analytic challenges that might arise for each feature.

Conclusions and Recommendations

The intent of this work is to inform the Army and DoD communities about whether, when, and how to usefully employ CEA and related metrics, including the CPE and CPO. In this section, we summarize the major findings of our research and offer recommendations for using and interpreting CEA and related metrics.

Findings on the Applicability of Cost-Effectiveness Analysis and Related Metrics

A comparison of the cost effectiveness—as opposed to the cost-per-unit—of different technologies can, at least theoretically, account for some of the differences in the technologies' capabilities, support costs, and other less direct costs of technology employment. However, CEA and related metrics, such as the CPE or CPO, are not sufficient for capturing all the salient features or aspects of all problem spaces. They can be more or less *feasible* and *useful* as tools to support decisionmaking, depending on the circumstances.

TABLE S.2
Framing a Technology Choice as a Cost-Effectiveness Analysis

Framing Feature	Specification Requirement	Analytic Challenges
Technology description	• Sufficiently clear description of the technologies—meaning the potential means for achieving the objective through performing some activities	• Existence of flexible and/or joint technologies

Objective (fixed, measurable)	• A fixed and measurable objective or set of comparable objectives that enables the normalization of benefits across technology options
	• Examples of objectives unrelated to strike might include
	  – increasing survivability of ground forces in an area
	  – executing a wet gap crossing
	  – disrupting enemy lodgment.
		• Lack of a singular, fixed, and measurable objective or set of comparable objectives
		• Risk or uncertainty around the context in which the objective must be achieved

Effects	• Effects are the immediate consequences of activities undertaken by the technologies that might contribute to meeting the objective.
	• Examples of effects unrelated to strike might include
	  – disabling or destroying enemy multiple rocket launchers
	  – suppressing enemy fires in a crossing area
	  – employing shore-to-ship fires to strike enemy maritime forces.
		• Feasibility of modeling effects at the level or with the realism required for assessing whether the objective has been met and for computing cost estimates
		• Data availability for necessary effect-modeling parameters

Costs	• Value of expended resources (explicit and implicit), including
	  – direct costs of munitions or other expenditures
	  – attrition costs
	  – support and other indirect costs
	  – rent[a]
		• Boundaries of the included cost elements
		• Data availability for the included cost elements

Ancillary benefits	• Positive results other than those directly related to the objective(s), meaning additional benefits of the technology that are not valued in the objective	• Existence of ancillary benefits • Lack of clarity on whether ancillary benefits should be considered as part of the objective or are decision-relevant • Data availability
Unintended consequences	• Negative results other than those directly related to the objective(s), such as drawbacks of the technology that do not prevent the technology from meeting the objective	• Existence of unintended consequences • Lack of clarity on whether unintended consequences should be considered as part of the objective or are decision-relevant • Data availability

[a] *Rent* is an implicit rate based on the marginal value of next best use other than in the strike mission.

In general, the less complex a problem or the less realistic the depiction of a problem, the easier it is to undertake an economic analysis, such as a CEA, and the more comprehensively a CPE, CPO, or other metric can summarize the information contained in the analysis. In particular, assessing cost effectiveness and developing associated metrics is most *feasible* when a specific set of conditions either holds for the problem at hand or can be treated as if it holds in a less realistic portrayal of the problem. The following conditions increase the feasibility of conducting a CEA and deriving related metrics:

- There is a single fixed and measurable objective—where fixed is defined as known, bounded, and unchanging—or a limited set of comparable objectives that is also fixed and measurable.
- There are relatively few (or minor) ancillary benefits and unintended consequences.
- The technologies being chosen from can operate independently.
- The context for achieving the objective is well understood by the decisionmaker and not highly variable.
- The boundaries of the problem space and cost elements lack ambiguity.
- The problem space and cost elements lack substantial risk or uncertainty.
- Sufficient data and computational capacity are available for conducting the analysis given the representation of the problem at hand.

Although these criteria might bear on all the forms of economic analysis, the first criterion, related to a single fixed and measurable objective, is especially important in a CEA because all the costs in a CEA must be assessed in relation to an objective. Thus, the further the problem veers from a single fixed and measurable objective, the more difficult the analysis becomes.

As an analytic representation moves far enough away from the underlying problem, the application of economic analysis might no longer answer the desired question. Therefore, we add that **conducting an economic analysis and developing associated metrics is most *useful* when the models used to represent the pursuit of the objective can incorporate sufficient realism to encompass the salient features of the problem space**. Although saliency matters for all forms of economic analysis, the set of real-world problems that can be aptly translated into a CEA and captured in its metrics might be smaller than it is for a CBA or BCA because CEA tends to be narrower.

Figure S.1 provides a notional depiction of our interpretation of the feasibility and usefulness of economic analysis, where *feasibility* refers to the technical ability to conduct an analysis or compute a related metric, and *usefulness* refers to whether or to what extent the analysis and metrics can meaningfully inform the decision. Many modeling exercises are technically possible, but not all of them will add value to a decisionmaking process.

FIGURE S.1
Feasibility and Usefulness of Economic Analysis

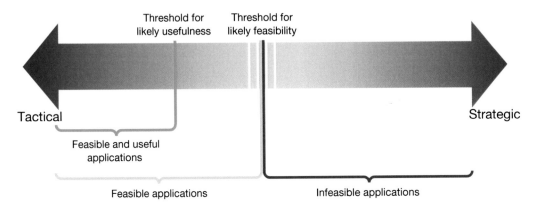

Furthermore, we find that making decisions based on a single metric can be risky, especially when **the results of an economic analysis are highly sensitive to modeling decisions and assumptions, with the results of a CEA being additionally sensitive to the definition of the objective**. Many such excursions would be required to fully understand the problem space and explore the impact of the assumptions made, presenting a significant need for modeling, costing, and assessment.

Finally, we reiterate that CEA and related metrics cannot speak to the question of whether the benefits of achieving an objective are worth (i.e., outweigh) the costs of achieving it, by any means, even if the analysis can identify a definitive cost-minimizing technology. Rather, a CEA can, at best, speak to the preferability of one option over others. Thus, we might imagine that the threshold for the likely usefulness of a CEA might be somewhat lower than for a CBA or BCA, but, because they can present additional analytical and data requirements, a CBA or BCA might be less feasible than a CEA.

Recommendations

Neither CEA nor any other form of economic analysis can universally provide the information needed to make the best decision across all acquisition and operational questions. Rather, the analysis, including any metrics that derive from it, can provide valuable information and insights under certain circumstances, and these circumstances can differ somewhat depending on the method of analysis. We provide the following recommendations for how analysts can use these findings to inform the development of future economic analyses:

- Analysts should consider whether they can *feasibly* meet the specification, computational, and data requirements for the type of economic analysis that they intend to pursue.
- Analysts should consider whether the *feasible* representation of the problem they have specified produces a *useful* economic analysis that can represent the salient features of the real-world problem.

- Analysts should refrain from relying solely on CEA and related CPE or CPO metrics when (1) the real-world problem cannot be portrayed reasonably with either a single fixed and measurable objective or a limited set of comparable objectives or (2) the real-world decision requires an assessment of net benefits.
- Analysts should consider the risks of using a single metric—such as a CPE, CPO, or net benefit estimate—for decision support.

Future work on the cost effectiveness of military capabilities should consider these limitations when both devising and applying results of economic analyses. Analysts should consider whether and how changes in assumptions or the extent of realism in an economic analysis affect the overall conclusions. Different assumptions about platform capabilities, adversary tactics, and future operating environments—and the level of uncertainty around these assumptions—could lead to different decisions, as could different assumptions about what to include in the costs. For a complex question of military technology choice, it might also be wise to work with a broader type of economic analysis (such as CBA or BCA) that can include disparate objectives and multiple metrics across a variety of assumptions and to complement quantitative assessments with more-qualitative information on the relative merits of the alternatives.

Contents

Figures and Tables

Figures

Tables

CHAPTER 1

Introduction

In July 2020, the Mitchell Institute for Aerospace Studies (the Mitchell Institute) published a report entitled *Resolving America's Defense Strategy-Resource Mismatch: The Case for Cost-per-Effect Analysis.*[1] The thesis of this report is that, given resource scarcity, the U.S. Air Force—and the U.S. Department of Defense (DoD) at large—should

> prioritize solutions that yield maximum mission value and not rely on overly simplistic metrics, like cheapest per-unit acquisition cost or individual cost-per flying hour, as these may actually drive more expensive, less capable solutions.[2]

The authors' recommended approach to that prioritization is to develop a metric that they call the "cost-per-effect" (CPE). The proposed CPE metric would measure "the sum of what it takes to net a desired mission result, not just a single system's acquisition and support costs without necessary context surrounding the capability's actual use."[3] Instead of computing simply a cost-per-unit (CPU) or cost-per-item for each technology alternative, a CPE metric would compare total costs for employing that technology to achieve a particular mission or *effect*. The preferred solution identified by such an approach would be not the least costly alternative *per unit* but the least costly alternative *per mission*, taking into account the differences in capabilities and enterprise-level costs among the alternatives.[4] Therefore, the authors' approach could incorporate variation in the potential capabilities of different solutions by normalizing over the desired effect.

To illustrate their approach, the authors show how a CPE metric can be used to value costly fifth-generation aircraft technologies, precision, and stealth. Cost-per-airframe metrics reveal extravagant costs of fifth-generation fighters compared with fourth-generation aircraft. Similarly, cost-per-munition metrics favor "dumb" munitions over advanced pre-

---

[1] David A. Deptula and Douglas A. Birkey, *Resolving America's Defense Strategy-Resource Mismatch: The Case for Cost-Per-Effect Analysis*, Mitchell Institute for Aerospace Studies, July 2020.

[2] Deptula and Birkey, 2020, p. 1.

[3] Deptula and Birkey, 2020, p. 1.

[4] By *enterprise-level costs*, we mean the cost of everything needed to achieve the objective(s). The Mitchell Institute report suggests that such costs should include mission costs, support costs, and even lifecycle ownership costs.

cision ones. The proposed CPE metric, on the other hand, accounts for the total resources required to complete a particular mission, which allows the metric to capture benefits of precision and stealth that are realized through reductions in the needed number of aircraft, likely aircraft attrition, and the cost of support and sustainment. The authors' applications of the approach illustrate the trade-off between acquisition and other costs: More advanced technology is generally more expensive per unit but possibly less costly on a per-mission basis. Beyond these applications, the authors suggest that this approach to analysis should be integrated into the existing Joint Capabilities Integration and Development System (JCIDS) process for making acquisition decisions and employed to make cross-service technology decisions, saying that

> [c]ost-per-effect assessments should also extend to other domain systems when deter-
> mining which approach yields the most favorable business case—i.e., ground-based long-
> range fires should be evaluated in parallel with their aerial and sea-based counterparts.[5]

Focusing on the overall costs of achieving objectives—rather than the per-unit costs of the systems that contribute to achieving those objectives—has intuitive appeal and the potential to contribute to more effective and efficient use of resources across the overall force. There is a long history of guidance in the federal government, including across DoD, that calls for economic analysis of resource allocation decisions and includes analytic methods—such as cost-effectiveness analysis (CEA), cost-benefit analysis (CBA), and business case analysis (BCA)—that are quite like those proposed in the Mitchell Institute report. Additionally, it appears as though DoD is considering the formalization of CPE metrics in its economic analysis toolkit: Section 147 of the 2021 National Defense Authorization Act calls on the Air Force to conduct a "study on the measures to assess cost-per-effect for key mission areas."[6]

In light of the Mitchell Institute report and related dialogues, the U.S. Army G-3/5/7 asked the RAND Arroyo Center to assess the feasibility and utility of a CPE metric as a potential tool for assessing costs and benefits in planned systems and capabilities development for the Army and other armed services. In this report, we first consider the available methods of economic analysis broadly and then focus on the theory and practice of relating costs to specific national security objectives and on deriving metrics from the analyses. Throughout this work, we have sought to identify challenges and opportunities for using both economic analyses and metrics in decisions about resource allocation. Our efforts center on what we would term *cost-effectiveness analysis* but which equates to a form of economic analysis that could serve as the basis for deriving the proposed CPE metrics contained in the Mitchell Institute report. Notwithstanding our emphasis on CEA and related metrics, many of the lessons drawn from our analytical efforts—including those regarding the difficulties of such

---

[5] Deptula and Birkey, 2020, p. 6.

[6] Public Law 116-283, William M. (Mac) Thornberry National Defense Authorization Act for Fiscal Year 2021; Section 147, Study on Measures to Assess Cost-per-Effect for Key Mission Areas, January 1, 2021.

efforts—also pertain to the other methods of economic analysis. Although a comprehensive comparison of all the methods (i.e., CEA, CBA, and BCA) is outside the scope of this report, we attempt to tease out important differences to better inform the Army and DoD communities about whether, when, and how to employ each method usefully.

Objective and Methods

To assess the feasibility and utility of a CPE metric, we first reviewed the small literature on CPE analysis and the larger literature on related forms of economic analysis, including CEA, that are used to support decisionmaking. Using the literature, we developed a theoretical framework for economic analysis that assesses cost effectiveness and yields a CPE-like metric. We then selected, in consultation with the sponsor, a notional battlefield example with which we could explore an application of economic analysis—specifically, CEA—by comparing the costs of several technology options for achieving a desired outcome. We applied the framework to the notional example qualitatively and drew additional insight from sample calculations that explored the effects of variation in the battlefield context, the presence of benefits and costs beyond the objective, the need to consider multiple objectives, and the inclusion and exclusion of various cost categories. Although we excluded the sample calculations from this report for sensitivity reasons, we present the theoretical framework, the qualitative application, and related insights for economic analysis in defense decisionmaking.

Overview of This Report

The rest of this document is organized as follows. In Chapter 2, we provide an overview of key concepts related to economic analysis. An understanding of these concepts and the various approaches to economic analysis and associated metric development sets the stage for a more detailed exploration of CEA and related metrics. In Chapter 3, we explore how the complexity of the *problem space*, which we define as the attributes or features of the real-world problem, and the degree of realism represented by the modeling effort contribute to the difficulty of an economic analysis. Whereas *complexity* refers to the intricacy of the real-world problem, *realism* refers to what we choose to capture in our analytic representation of the real-world problem. In that chapter, we focus on CEA but also consider how complexity and realism can impart more, less, or different types of difficulty, depending on the method of economic analysis applied and the metrics derived. In Chapter 4, we revisit the concepts introduced in Chapters 2 and 3 more concretely with our notional battlefield example. In Chapter 5, we lay out our major conclusions and recommendations regarding the use of CEA and related metrics.

Finally, we provide three technical appendixes with additional information. In Appendix A, we provide a glossary of terms used in our discussions of economic analysis and in our approach to CEA. In Appendix B, we present a generalized depiction of CEA, including different sources of complexity, in a series of figures. Finally, in Appendix C, we show how the concept of real option value can be used to understand the value of flexibility in an economic analysis.

CHAPTER 2

An Introduction to Economic Analysis

Recent interest in measuring CPE has emerged from a tradition of economic analysis in the U.S. national security community that extends back at least as far as the mid-20th century, with work on CEA at DoD and at the RAND Corporation,[1] but it can be traced to much earlier efforts in other venues. One historian of economic analysis credits the Rivers and Harbor Act of 1902 with "the first systematic attempt to apply cost-benefit analysis to government economic decisions" but also describes a failed attempt to introduce economic analysis to a choice between steel and cast-iron rifles in the late 1800s and the use of economic analysis in a massive construction project in 11th century China.[2]

For today's U.S. defense context, Department of Defense Instruction (DoDI) 7041.03 defines *economic analysis* as "[a] systematic approach to the problem of choosing the best method of allocating scarce resources to achieve a given *objective*" (emphasis added) and "includes consideration of costs, benefits, risk, and uncertainty."[3] Economic analysis applies to a broad variety of resource allocation decisions including, but not limited to, those involving "startup research, acquisition, renewal, renovation, conversion, upgrade, expansion, pre-planned product improvement, leasing, or operations of all programs or projects."[4] DoDI 7041.03 presumes the decision results in a commitment, in which a series of expenditures and benefits accrues beyond a program or project's inception, but we can apply the principles of weighing costs, benefits, risks, and uncertainty to other forms of operational commitments, including those of strategies and tactics. DoDI 7041.03, Army guidance,[5] and other

---

[1] See, for example, Alain Enthoven, "How Systems Analysis, Cost-Effectiveness Analysis, or Benefit-Cost Analysis First Became Influential in Federal Government Program Decision-Making," *Journal of Benefit Cost Analysis*, Vol. 10, No. 2, Summer 2019; Francois Melese, Anke Richter, and Binyam Solomon, "Introduction: Military Cost-Benefit Analysis," in Francois Melese, Anke Richter, and Binyam Solomon, eds., *Military Cost-Benefit Analysis: Theory and Practice*, Routledge, 2015; and E. S. Quade, "A History of Cost Effectiveness," RAND Corporation, P-4557, 1971.

[2] Quade, 1971, pp. 4, 5–7, and 9.

[3] DoD, *Economic Analysis for Decision-Making*, Department of Defense Instruction 7041.03, September 9, 2015, incorporating change 1, October 2, 2017, p. 18.

[4] DoD, 2017, p. 1.

[5] Department of the Army Pamphlet 415–3 similarly defines economic analysis in the context of construction projects as a "structured method to identify, analyze, and compare costs and benefits of the alternatives" (Headquarters, Department of the Army, *Economic Analysis: Description and Methods*, Department

federal guidance point to CEA, CBA, and BCA as different methods for conducting economic analysis and, thus, suggest treating *economic analysis* as an umbrella term that encompasses a variety of analytical methods.

In the rest of this chapter, we first introduce three methods of economic analysis: CBA, CEA, and BCA. Other forms of economic analysis can be applied to defense-oriented decisions about allocating resources, but these three provide a well-trodden starting point for understanding how to approach such decisions. Next, we consider the limitations of metrics that can derive from or contribute to those methods. In the decades following DoD's turn to economic analysis, DoD practitioners and RAND researchers noted challenges working with standard economic methods, including CEA, and the metrics they yield. For example, the practitioners and researchers called out challenges related to computational requirements, data availability, and interpretation, most of which are still relevant today and bear on the analysis that we develop in this report. Finally, we discuss how the nature of the *problem space*, defined as the features or attributes of the real-world problem, can affect the form of the analytical solution to the economic analysis. For our use of technical vocabulary in this discussion and in later chapters, see Appendix A.

Understanding Methods of Economic Analysis

In this section, we draw from contemporary sources to characterize CBA, CEA, and BCA, paying particular attention to the techniques that each method employs, the metrics that each method can generate or use, and, especially, the kinds of questions each method can answer.[6] We acknowledge that others have used or might still use the same terms in different ways. Over time and across communities, different researchers, policy analysts, and practitioners have characterized the methods of economic analysis differently, depending partly on the circumstances and focus of their interests. For example, some policy analysts with a greater interest in cost effectiveness have described CBA as a subset of CEA; others with a greater interest in balancing costs and benefits have described CEA as a subset of CBA.[7]

---

of the Army Pamphlet 415–3, September 28, 2018, p. 4). The pamphlet specifies the first step in the analytical process as establishing a project objective: "The project objective is a problem statement, which defines the need the Government is attempting to answer. The reason for undertaking an [economic analysis] is to discern the most beneficial means of achieving a solution to a perceived problem. The project objective must be an unbiased statement of the problem, or project need" (Headquarters, Department of the Army, 2018, p. 6).

[6] We define *contemporary* as either recent or current, depending on the source, because some current formal guidance on economic analysis, such as that from the Office of Management and Budget (OMB), dates back 20 years or more.

[7] Quade (1971, p. 3), for example, describes CBA as "a specialized form of cost-benefit analysis" and argues that the differences in methods are largely a matter of emphasis.

Cost-Benefit Analysis

In a CBA, both the costs and the benefits of meeting an objective are monetized insomuch as possible, which enables the derivation of a *net benefit* (i.e., the monetary value of the benefits minus the monetary value of the costs) for any means of meeting an objective.[8] (Table 2.1 summarizes these points, assuming that the monetary value is expressed in dollars.) The net benefit—typically evaluated as a *net present value* if costs and benefits accrue over time—constitutes the primary metric of the analysis and can be used (1) to decide whether a weapon system, program, strategy, or tactic, is *worth it* (i.e., whether the benefits outweigh the costs) and (2) as a basis for making comparisons not just among different paths to pursuing the same objectives but also among different paths leading to different, potentially disparate, objectives. For example, if the Army were deciding whether to allocate resources to one of two different types of weapon systems, it could compare the net benefits of each system (even if the Army would use the systems to serve entirely different purposes). That is, the Army could ask where its spending would yield the greatest net benefit. At yet higher levels of government, policymakers could use CBA to compare the merits of spending on national security with spending to address unrelated societal concerns by framing all such spending in terms of the dollar value of its net benefits. That said, like DoDI 7041.03, we focus in this report on comparisons of different means of obtaining the same objective, all in the national security domain.

Cost-Effectiveness Analysis

In a CEA, the costs are represented monetarily, but the benefits are represented in other nonmonetary units or qualitatively.[9] For example, the benefits could be represented as the attainment of a particular effect, such as destroying a target, or meeting a broader objective, such as disabling an adversary or prevailing in battle. However, fixing the benefits in this way (as attaining an effect or meeting an objective) has implications for the types of questions that a CEA—and its metrics—can answer, which we address below.

A CEA can generate a metric, such as a CPE or CPO, consisting of a ratio that is expressed in terms of dollars per unit of the effect or objective, respectively.[10] A CPO metric, so defined, might be better aligned with DoD's guidance on economic analysis, which refers broadly to *objectives*, than a CPE metric, which could be construed as somewhat narrower in our parlance (if not in the parlance of the Mitchell Institute's report). Consider, for example, the difference between disabling an adversary (an *objective*) and destroying a target (an *effect*). The *effect* might contribute to the *objective*, but it would be just a stepping stone—or part of a larger initiative—to reaching the objective.

---

[8] See, for example, OMB, *Regulatory Analysis*, Circular A-4, September 17, 2003.

[9] See, for example, OMB, 2003.

[10] In some cases, many of which we explore in this report, a problem can be reduced to *cost minimization* (i.e., choosing the least costly means of obtaining an outcome).

TABLE 2.1

Comparison of Methods of Economic Analysis

Characteristic	CBA	CEA	BCA
Techniques	• Evaluate monetary costs, monetary benefits, ancillary benefits, unintended consequences, and risks of investment, tactics, strategy, programs, etc. that can meet objective(s)	• Evaluate monetary costs, ancillary benefits, unintended consequences, and risks of meeting objective(s) through investment, tactics, strategy, programs, etc.	• Various techniques (e.g., CBA, CEA, break-even analysis, and financial analysis)
Metrics (units)	• Net benefits (monetary *level*) are the results of the analysis • Mean, variance, CPU (monetary *ratio*) can inform the analysis	• CPE, CPO (monetary *ratio*) are the results of the analysis • Mean, variance, CPU (monetary *ratio*) can inform the analysis	• Various metrics (e.g., net benefits, CPE, CPO, CPU, ROI) can emerge from or inform the analysis
Decision rules	• Net benefits > 0 • Choose alternative with the most net benefit (maximum), subject to ancillary benefits, unintended consequences, risks, uncertainties, and other factors	• Choose alternative with the least cost (minimum), subject to ancillary benefits, unintended consequences, risks, uncertainties, and other factors	• Differ by technique(s)
Uses	• Establishing *admissibility* (Is it worth it?) and *preferability* (Is it better?) • Comparing alternatives for addressing the same or disparate objectives	• Establishing preferability but not admissibility • Comparing alternatives for addressing the same objective	• Differ by technique(s)
Information needs	• Costs, benefits • Monetary values of costs and benefits	• Costs, benefits • Monetary value of costs, but not of benefits	• Differ by technique(s)

NOTE: In cases that fall between these depictions of CBA and CEA, it might be possible to partially monetize benefits. CPO = cost-per-objective; ROI = return on investment.

The CPE and CPO metrics that derive from the analysis can be used to support comparisons of alternatives for pursuing the same effect or objective. (For example, it might take $100 million to disable the adversary with one weapon system but $150 million with another.) However, these metrics cannot be used to answer as many kinds of questions as can the net benefits that derive from a CBA. Specifically, these metrics cannot be used to compare alternatives that are intended to meet disparate goals, such as those on national security and social policy, unless the goals can be distilled to a common unit of measure.[11] Furthermore, a CEA

---

[11] This would require reframing the objectives (e.g., disabling an adversary and reducing toxic emissions) for equivalence. For example, the ultimate goals of both disabling the adversary, on the one hand, and

cannot take a stand on inherent worth but, rather, presumes that meeting the objective is *worth it*—or that it has been preselected as worthwhile or necessary by a prior decisionmaking process—and, by extension, that the most cost-effective way of meeting the objective is also worth it. It is possible that, if one could calculate the net benefits of taking action, these values would be negative. Moreover, a cost ratio, such as CPE or CPO, can be hard to interpret or even misleading when, for example, one weapon system can yield *more* or *less* of an effect than another, which is a point that we return to below.

Business Case Analysis

BCA has been defined as "a decision support tool that projects the likely financial results and other business consequences of an action" and that might take a more "enterprise wide" or "holistic" view of the effects of the action than a CBA or CEA.[12] The author goes on to say that "[a] good business case, like a legal case, uses evidence and reasoning to reach a conclusion."[13] The analysis might both use and produce various financial and economic metrics, including those that are incorporated into or emanate from a CBA or CEA. For example, a BCA could augment a net present value estimate from a CBA by presenting other financial indicators that pertain to ROI.[14] As might be said of any form of economic analysis, the costs and benefits in a BCA will depend on how the analyst designs the business case: "[C]osts and benefits do not exist—they are not defined—until the case is designed."[15] This implies that the design—which starts with a premise regarding a purpose for allocating resources and reflects decisions about the scope and other attributes of the analysis—sets the stage for everything that follows.[16] Simply put, the costs, the benefits, and, ultimately, the results

---

reducing toxic emissions, on the other hand, could be saving lives. In that case, the results of a comparative analysis of the costs of a weapon system that disables an adversary and a program that reduces toxic emissions could be measured in terms of mortality avoidance and, at least hypothetically, compared on that basis.

[12] Marty J. Schmidt, *The Business Case Guide*, 2nd ed., Solution Matrix, 2002, p. 1. The *DoD Product Support Business Case Analysis Guidebook* does not draw a sharp distinction between BCA and other forms of economic analysis but rather seems to equate them by saying that "[o]ther names for a BCA are Economic Analysis, Cost-Benefit Analysis, and Benefit-Cost Analysis." However, the guidebook also suggests that a BCA might encompass more enterprise wide and holistic concerns than other such decision support tools (Office of the Assistant Secretary of Defense for Logistics and Materiel Readiness, *DoD Product Support Business Case Analysis Guidebook*, U.S. Department of Defense, 2014, p. 5).

[13] Schmidt, 2002, p. 2.

[14] In addition to Schmidt, 2002, see Raymond Sheen and Amy Gallo, *HBR Guide to Building Your Business Case*, Harvard Business Review, July 7, 2015; and Frank Camm, John Matsumura, Lauren A. Mayer, and Kyle Siler-Evans, *A New Methodology for Conducting Product Support Business Case Analysis (BCA): With Illustrations from the F-22 Product Support BCA*, RAND Corporation, RR-1664-AF, 2017.

[15] Schmidt, 2002, p. 5.

[16] Schmidt, 2002, p. 5. Similarly, Sheen and Gallo (2015, pp. 3–6) emphasize the primacy of establishing the problem or "business need."

depend on the question we ask (and the assumptions we make and limitations we impose when we try to answer it).

Summary Comments on CBA, CEA, and BCA

In our articulation of these forms of economic analysis, which stipulate an objective,[17] the main distinction between CBA and CEA lies in the extent of monetization. BCA stands somewhat apart as a tool—or toolkit—that can include or build on elements of each of the other methods. (Table 2.1 summarizes our comparison of these methods.) Of special note, CBA can be used to address questions of worth (e.g., Is an alternative worth it?) and to inform resource allocation decisions among disparate objectives because the analysis monetizes costs and benefits, whereas CEA presupposes worth and can be used only to choose among alternatives for meeting the same objective. That said, a CBA can present its own challenges, for example, when fully realizing its potential requires monetizing benefits that are hard to monetize. Consider, for example, the difficulty of assigning a dollar value to prevailing in battle or disabling an adversary. A BCA might take the broadest view of any of these methods by incorporating elements of each method and drawing on others, but it might, if adopted to its fullest, require the most analytical effort and data. However, regardless of the method, be it a CBA, CEA, or BCA, the analyst would still need to consider the potential for *ancillary benefits* and *unintended consequences*—additional good or bad results that are not part of the objective, such as less attrition or more casualties, respectively—as well as any *risks* or *uncertainties* associated with the problem, all of which we discuss in detail in later chapters and appendixes.[18]

Understanding the Limitations of Different Metrics

In this section, we review the main differences in the metrics associated with each method of economic analysis (Table 2.1) and discuss some of the analytical implications of those differences. First, we introduce the CPU metric—a metric that often takes center stage in public discourse—and address its interpretation in relation to CPE and CPO metrics. Next, we consider the properties of CPE and CPO metrics, both on their own and in relation to net benefits.[19] We start with the CPU metric and build to the other metrics because the CPU is

---

[17] DoD, 2017.

[18] OMB (2003) refers to "ancillary benefits," on the one hand, and, interchangeably, "undesirable side effects," "countervailing risks," and "adverse consequence," on the other hand, but the literature often uses the term "unintended consequences" to refer to the latter, even if it can include the former. Thus, whereas unintended consequences could be positive or negative, we use the term to refer to only negative consequences.

[19] We refer to both CPO and CPE metrics, but we focus more on CPE metrics in the examples in this section, both because interest in CPE metrics motivated our research and because we can draw general obser-

the simplest among them. As much as drawing insight from a CPE or CPO metric can present analytical challenges, which we discuss below, we find that drawing insight from unit costs with a CPU metric can be harder still.

In essence, a CPU metric is the "price tag" for an item, such as a weapon system, without any regard to its effect or an objective, whereas a CPE or CPO metric is the price tag for the effect or objective, respectively, that an item can be used to achieve. A CPU metric could, for example, capture an item's acquisition cost, life-cycle cost, leasing cost, or, even, employment cost—such as a cost-per-shot—but without concern for what the item produces.

Comparing costs by systems, as in the case of a CPU metric, means that both costs and effects or objectives can differ by alternative but without the analysis considering those differences. In Figure 2.1, we see that the small cannon costs less than the big cannon, but it also delivers less capability for that cost.[20] Moreover, not only could the systems produce different *amounts* of something—as the cannons do in Figure 2.1, where both cannons can destroy the same kind of target—but they could also produce different *somethings*. By contrast, normalizing on effects—as with the CPE metric in that figure—can facilitate an apples-to-apples comparison, albeit subject to the limitations that we discuss in the next few paragraphs. In Figure 2.1, the small cannon can destroy just one target at a cost of $100 per target, and the large cannon can destroy two targets at a cost of $75 per target. The CPE for the large cannon

FIGURE 2.1

Comparison of CPU and CPE Metrics

CPU is the price tag for an item
- Numerator is the cost of items
- Denominator counts the items (e.g., systems)
- Comparing costs per item (e.g., system) means both costs and effects can differ because different items can yield different effects
- Provides information for economic analysis

CPE is the price tag for an effect
- Numerator is the cost of effects
- Denominator counts the effects
- Comparing costs by normalizing on effects instead of items generates the cost per instance of an effect or suite of effects
- Derives from economic analysis

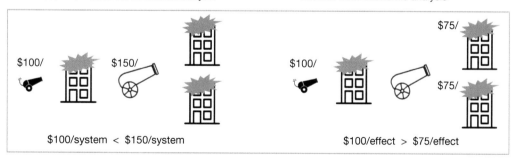

$100/system < $150/system $100/effect > $75/effect

vations from relatively simple diagrams. Later in this report, we turn to objectives and demonstrate the use of economic analysis, specifically, CEA, to relate costs to a specific objective and to derive a CPO metric. For a series of more complicated yet still generic diagrams of CEA in relation to various objectives, see Appendix B.

[20] In this simple example, we are not distinguishing costs in any precise manner, but we could think of the cost as a *cost-per-system*, as shown in Figure 2.1, or as a *cost-per-shot*.

would be $25 less than the CPE for the small cannon, suggesting that it might be a better value. Still, if we wanted to destroy only a single target, the small cannon might be preferable because the extra damage would not yield any gains.

Turning to CPE and CPO metrics, we noted previously that these metrics cannot be used to answer as many questions as can the net benefit from a CBA and, even in their more-limited use, that they can present interpretative challenges. Whereas an analysis of net benefits can tell us whether one allocation of resources is *better* than another and whether any allocation is *worth it*, CPO and CPE metrics can, at best, tell us only whether one allocation is better than another.[21] These metrics also present interpretive challenges because they, like a CPU metric, are ratios. By normalizing on the effect or objective, they can enable apples-to-apples comparisons, but by focusing on the cost of obtaining just a unit of effect or an objective, these metrics can be misleading and could result in the user choosing the wrong alternative. That is, an alternative might look appealing based on a comparison of metrics from a CEA, but the net benefit of the alternative, had it been calculable in a CBA, might have been relatively small.[22]

Whether a ratio, such as a CPE or CPO metric, can reliably determine preferability hinges largely on the scalability of the problem.[23] To be more concrete, we can return to the cannons in Figure 2.1 and, with slightly different numbers, show how valuing the effect (i.e., the destruction of a target) to calculate a net benefit can lead to a different answer depending on which elements of the problem are scalable.[24] Specifically, we increase the cost of the large cannon to $225 without any improvement in performance (implying a new CPE of $112.50), we hold the costs and performance of the small cannon constant, we value the destruction of each target at $1,000, and we vary our assumptions about scalability.

First, we consider a choice in which the technologies, their effects, and the related costs and benefits are all linearly scalable. In this case, we could work with two small cannons at a cost of $100 each (implying a total cost of $200) or one large cannon at a cost of $225 to produce the same amount of effects and yield the same amount of benefits (i.e., we could destroy two buildings at a value of $1,000 each).[25] In this case, when we normalize on effects

---

[21] The added insight of the net benefit comes at a price because calculating a net benefit requires more information (i.e., the dollar value of benefits) than does calculating a CPE or CPO.

[22] Earlier, we suggested the possibility that the net benefit of an action could be negative, but here we are just suggesting that a comparison of net benefits from a CBA would suggest a different ranking.

[23] This result is well documented in the public finance literature (e.g., Harvey S. Rosen, *Public Finance*, 6th ed., McGraw-Hill, 2001, p. 220), as when a small investment offers a higher rate of return than a large investment but the net present value of the large investment exceeds that of the small investment, and in regulatory guidance (OMB, 2003, p. 10).

[24] As we will demonstrate, in a fully *linearly scalable problem* (i.e., one in which we can increase or decrease the amount of any technology or effect and the associated costs and benefits rise and fall proportionally with each incremental unit of change), the answers from a CEA and CBA should be the same.

[25] When the technology, effects, costs, and benefits scale linearly, we can increase the number of small cannons to match the large cannon effect for effect, at a constant cost-per-cannon and value-per-effect.

in the CPE calculation, the small cannon looks like the better deal. When we calculate the net benefits, as we would in a CBA, the small cannon still looks like a better deal. The CPE for the small and large cannons would be $100 and $112.50, respectively. The net benefit of two small cannons would be $1,800 ($2,000 minus $200), and the net benefit of one large cannon would be $1,775 ($2,000 minus $225). Thus, the small cannon would be the better choice by either measure.

Second, we consider a choice in which we cannot scale the technologies but in which additional effects still convey additional value, such that destroying two targets is twice as valuable as destroying one.[26] Now, when we normalize on effects in the CPE calculation, the small cannon looks like the better deal, but when we calculate the net benefits, as we would in a CBA, it does not. The CPE of the large cannon ($112.50) would still be $12.50 higher than the CPE of the small cannon ($100). However, if we value the effects at $1,000 per target, the net benefit of the large cannon would exceed that of the small cannon, even though the CPE is higher. The net benefit of the large cannon would be $1,775 ($2,000 minus $225), but the net benefit of the small cannon would be $900 ($1,000 minus $100), suggesting that the large cannon would represent a better value than the small cannon.

Third, if the effects are not scalable—meaning that destroying a second (or a third or fourth) target is irrelevant or impossible and, hence, valueless—then regardless of whether the technologies are scalable, a net benefit calculation would also point to the small cannon. In this case, the net benefit of the small cannon would be $900 ($1,000 minus $100), but the net benefit of the large cannon would be just $775 ($1,000 minus $225).

More generally, ratio- or rate-based metrics, such as a CPE or CPO metric, can make more sense in fully scalable circumstances than in others. For example, in the third case, in which a single fixed effect was all that mattered, a cost-minimization exercise (as discussed in the next section) might serve as a more appropriate tool for comparing options. In such a case, which we might treat as representing a relatively simple application of CEA to a resource allocation decision, the CPE or CPO metric is just the cost of obtaining the effect or meeting the objective by each technology, and we can select the technology that is least costly.[27]

Lastly, we note that, although the CPU metric might provide a relatively weak basis for choosing among alternative resource allocations, it can play an important part in budgeting exercises—for example, purchase costs require financing—and can be an essential input to other types of analysis, including CBA, CEA, and BCA. That is, to assess the costs of the alternatives in those analyses, we might need information about unit costs. For example, if the analysis involves a purchase decision, we would need to know the unit prices of the items under consideration to assess their net benefits (CPEs, CPOs, ROIs, etc.). The "Metrics" row

---

[26] This could be described as the extreme case of nonlinearity, in which the cost of a second small cannon is infinitely high. Alternatively, we could have framed this as a choice between two weapon systems in which one system is more efficient than the other but also has less capacity than the other.

[27] Strictly speaking, the cost of obtaining the effect or meeting the objective is still a ratio insomuch as it is the price of something, hence a price tag, and any such price tag is a ratio.

in Table 2.1 indicates potential roles for CPU, CPO, and CPE metrics in each form of economic analysis, along with their units of measure.

Understanding the Problem Space

In some instances, it could be possible to reduce an economic analysis to a cost-minimization problem (i.e., selecting the least costly alternative), but that will depend largely on the nature of the problem space, defined as the attributes or features of the real-world problem, including the objective. Figure 2.2 shows that greater complexity, defined as the intricacy of the problem space, makes it progressively harder to choose among alternatives, such as different weapon systems, just by selecting an approach that minimzes the cost of success. As we move toward the right in Figure 2.2, the objective—hence, the meaning of success—is harder to pin down. Different approaches to meeting the objective can also entail ancillary benefits, unintended consequences, and uncertainty about the objective, approach, or operating environment. Furthermore, the technologies in question can present complications of their own, as when multiple weapon systems must be used together or one weapon system can yield more than one objective. The problem spaces that are most amenable to cost mimimization would feature a single *fixed* (i.e., known, bounded, and unchanging) and measurable objective—such as destroying a specific number of enemy targets—with no ancillary benefits, unintended consequences, risks, etc. By contrast, the problem spaces that might be the least amenable could feature multiple *fluid* (i.e., unknown, unbounded, or changing) objectives, various difficult-to-quantify ancillary benefits and unintended consequences, and uncertainty about many parameters of the decision.[28] Arguably, the simplest cases are likely to be the narrowest, most tactically oriented, and the most complex cases are likely to be the broadest, most strategically oriented.

---

[28] An objective is *bounded* if it has clear, accepted limits (see Appendix A).

FIGURE 2.2

Cost Minimization in the Problem Space Continuum

**Set of decisions
more/most amenable
to cost minimization**

**Set of decisions
less/least amenable
to cost minimization**

A continuum related to the complexity of the problem space

More fixity and less ancillary
benefits, unintended
consequences, risk, etc.

Less fixity and more ancillary
benefits, unintended
consequences, risk, etc.

Decreasing complexity

Increasing complexity

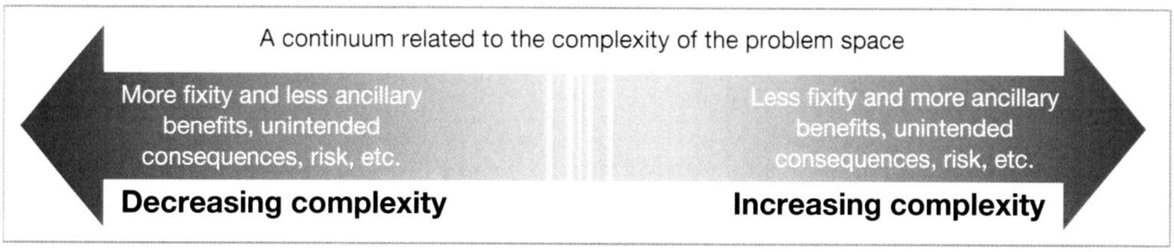

Most amenable

- Single fixed and measurable objective
- No ancillary benefits or unintended consequences
- No risks
- Separable technologies

Cases in between

- Single unfixed, but still measurable, objective
- Quantifiable ancillary benefits or unintended consequences
- Quantifiable risks
- Separable technologies

Least amenable

- Multiple unfixed and unmeasurable objectives
- Nonquantifiable ancillary benefits or unintended consequences
- Uncertainty
- Joint technologies

CHAPTER 3

Generalizing Cost-Effectiveness Analysis

In this chapter, we explore how conducting an economic analysis, including a CEA, can become more difficult in problem spaces that are more complex or depicted with greater realism. Whereas *complexity* refers to the intricacy of the real-world problem, *realism* refers to what we choose to capture in our analytic representation of the real-world problem. Stated differently, complexity is baked into the problem space, but realism is a choice. When we increase or decrease the realism of our analysis, we are not changing the *problem space*, per se, but how or with how much fidelity we depict it. Although complexity and realism are distinct concepts, they are related because the greater the complexity of a problem space, the harder it might be to portray it realistically.

Complexity has many possible sources, which we discuss throughout this chapter, but one noteworthy source is the level of analysis—be it an engagement, the battlefield, or a campaign—at which we specify the objective. Furthermore, this level of analysis can serve as a driver of other sources of complexity. For example, as we move from engagement to battlefield to campaign, we might find it harder to pin down a single fixed and measurable objective, and we might face greater risk or uncertainty in the operating environment. Other sources of complexity, such as those relating to the capabilities of a weapon system or the emergence of ancillary benefits and unintended consequences, might not progress similarly.

The extent of realism in the analysis can also affect its difficulty; decisions about realism need to weigh the technical feasibility of modeling capabilities and data availability against analytic need because some questions require greater resolution than others. Costing can also become more difficult as realism increases because more realism might require breaking out more types of costs and more precision around each cost component. Challenges related to adding realism to an analysis generally increase with the complexity of the problem space, and, for any given problem space, adding realism can make the exercise more difficult and might involve more fully acknowledging complexity.

Figure 3.1 illustrates the difficulty of generalizing CEA in relation to the *level* and *realism* of the analysis. The least difficult applications reside at the bottom left, corresponding to the narrowest and most stylized applications, and the most difficult applications reside at the top right, corresponding to the broadest and least stylized applications:

- As we move up an arrow, we can hold the objective constant but seek increasingly greater realism so that the analytical challenges would relate more to the limits of modeling

FIGURE 3.1

The Difficulty of Generalizing Cost-Effectiveness Analysis and Deriving Related Metrics in Relation to Realism and the Level of Analysis

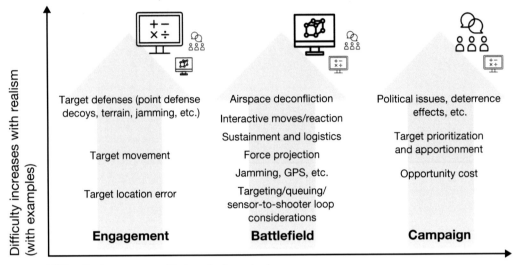

NOTE: The representations of mathematical operations (a computer with addition, subtraction, multiplication, and division signs), simulations (a computer with a model cube), and expert judgement (individuals with thought bubbles), chart the increasing difficulty of conducting analyses across levels. GPS = Global Positioning System.

capabilities and data availability than to our conceptualization of the objective, potential ancillary benefits and unintended consequences, risks, etc.

- As we move across the arrows, the difficulty of the application derives from the scope of the underlying question, which increases with each level (i.e., from engagement to battlefield to campaign). The flow from left to right also suggests a shift from tactically to strategically oriented questions. Still, we cannot divorce the analytical challenges of scope and realism because the difficulty of the modeling exercise, the need for data, and, in some instances, the need for professional judgment might grow as we move from left to right.

In Figure 3.1, we use cartoon-like representations of mathematical operations, simulations, and expert judgment at the top of each arrow to indicate the type of analysis that might dominate in each level. Basic mathematical operations dominate the left-most arrow, representing the relative ease of modeling just an engagement. Expert judgment, depicted with thought bubbles, dominates the right-most arrow to suggest the need to rely on assumptions, and, by extension, professional expertise, because of the difficulty of modeling the salient aspects of a problem at the campaign level. The computer symbol at the top of the middle arrow represents the need for more-sophisticated simulation or modeling exercises in this middle space. The concepts represented on each of the three arrows provide examples of the types of things that we might choose to include in the analysis as we increase the realism with which we depict the problem space, some of which might be capturable only by using sophisticated simulation (e.g., interactive moves) or expert judgment (e.g., deterrence effects). Whereas technical feasibility might present the most-salient constraints as we move up the arrows, expanding the scope with each level might also demand a more powerful model, additional data, or more reliance on assumptions and the professional judgment of modelers, analysts, and others.

In the rest of this chapter, we explore how generalizing CEA—and, by extension, deriving related metrics—becomes more difficult when we face more complexity or try to insert greater realism into our analysis. We devote particular attention to objectives, technology, context, risk, and uncertainty and to setting boundaries for estimating costs. In each case, we are considering complexity and realism in relation to analyses that

- describe paths that lead from technologies to various effects and, eventually, to results that meet one or more objectives
- estimate costs that accrue along those paths
- calculate metrics, such as a CPO metric, for those paths.

Choosing a technology, such as the mix of weapon systems, amounts to a resource allocation decision that will establish a path to the objective or objectives and incur different types of costs. For visual renderings that capture this representation of the economic analysis, see Appendix B, where we draw paths from technologies to objectives that illustrate different sources of complexity and explore the implications of the complexity for conducting economic analyses, including CEA.

Throughout this chapter, we are not arguing for an ideal amount of complexity or realism; rather, we are exploring how working in a more complex problem space or choosing to model a problem space more realistically, *as the question at hand necessitates*, can make the analysis more difficult or, in some instances, reduce our confidence in the answer. If working in a more complex problem space or adding realism to an analysis increases our reliance on assumptions and professional judgment, we might have less confidence in our findings, depending on how much the assumptions and judgment matter to our findings.

Sources of Complexity in the Problem Space

As Figures 2.2 and 3.1 suggest, complexity can exist along a continuum, from least to most complex, but also in relation to many different aspects of the problem space, not least of which is the specification of the objective. In the simplest analytical cases, we might consider a single fixed and measurable objective—such as destroying a set number of enemy targets—and neither the objective nor the means of obtaining it would present discernable ancillary benefits, unintended consequences, risks, uncertainties, technological interrelatedness, or temporal, spatial, or other dynamics. Other increasingly complex circumstances might involve multiple objectives, either fixed or fluid; various ancillary benefits; unintended consequences; and others.

Box 3.1 provides a typology of sources of complexity that we refer to in the discussion that follows. Although we parse the sources cleanly in Box 3.1, we acknowledge that they can be interconnected and reinforcing, as was apparent in our discussion of the level of analysis and will be apparent in this discussion.

BOX 3.1
Typology of Sources of Complexity

The simplest analytical cases involve problem spaces with more fixity, on the one hand, and fewer ancillary benefits, unintended consequences, risks, uncertainties, and interrelated technologies, on the other hand. Here, we set out a typology of sources of complexity, but, despite our seemingly clean parsing, acknowledge that the sources of complexity are sometimes interconnected and reinforcing.

- Specification of objectives
  - Number of objectives
    - Level(s) of objectives (i.e., engagement, battlefield, or campaign)
    - Potential for sequential or nested objectives, meaning that one objective must precede another or that multiple objectives contribute to another
    - Weighting or combining objectives
  - Fixity of objectives
  - Constraints on attaining objectives
- Relevance of ancillary benefits or unintended consequences
- Nature of technology that produces effects, such as
  - A weapon system that might be able to support more than one objective
  - A weapon system that might depend on support from or cooperation with others
  - Different features of a weapon system that might hold different values in different use cases
- Types of contexts under consideration
  - Behavioral (e.g., strategic or nonstrategic) characteristics
  - Nonbehavioral (e.g., temporal [single- or multiperiod], physical, spatial, or other environmental) characteristics
- Designation of boundaries on costs, effects, and other phenomena
  - Drawing a circle around the problem space
  - Defining effects and contributions to effects
- Risks or uncertainties with respect to any or all of the above

The Objective

The simplest objectives are singular, fixed, and measurable, but we can readily imagine departures from this simplicity. First, we consider the potential for multiple—but still fixed and measurable—objectives that can occur at one or more levels of analysis. Then, we consider the possibility of one or more fluid or hard-to-measure objectives. Lastly, we consider the potential for constraints on objectives or, by extension, the paths to meeting them.

Multiple Fixed and Measurable Objectives

Multiple fixed and measurable objectives can occur at the same level of analysis (such as an engagement) or they can span multiple levels (reaching from engagement to battlefield to campaign), and they can impart varying degrees of complexity. When multiple objectives occur at the same level, as within an engagement, but have no bearing on each other or the resource allocation decision, the problem might be as simple as an equivalent number of single fixed and measurable objectives.[1] However, when one objective leads to another sequentially, either at the same level or across levels, or involves some bundling, the problem can be harder to solve. For example, meeting the objectives for a series of related engagements by destroying specific numbers of targets in each engagement, could, together, contribute to meeting a larger battlefield objective, such as stopping the advance of an adversary.

In Appendix B, we show how incorporating a second level of *nested* objectives—as might reach from a set of engagements to the battlefield or even as far as a campaign—can result in having to consider many feasible paths and introduces the possibility of seeking effects that might not lead directly to an immediate, lower-level objective but that can contribute to the ultimate objective. Still, even with the large number of paths, the set of solutions shrinks quickly through pairwise comparisons of costs. We find that *if* we know where we need to go and *if* we can trace the paths to getting there, we can reduce the decision to a relatively simple cost-minimization problem, *assuming* we can estimate the costs for each path.

However, the above caveats are not insubstantial. The sequential problem requires a *forward-looking solution* (i.e., one that accounts for the full length of the path to the ultimate objective and, as we discuss later in the section, any mounting risks or uncertainties along that path).[2] The longer the path from a technology to an objective, the more difficulty one might expect to have tracing it and obtaining the data to support it, which, in turn, might suggest greater reliance on assumptions and professional judgment. Even with good data on the properties of the technologies and their intended effects, the need for assumptions, such as those regarding the operating environment and costs, might grow with the path.

The analysis could be even more challenging if the objectives at one level are not equally important or, with sequential or nested objectives, contribute differently to meeting an overarching objective on another level. Some targets might matter more than others in attempting

---

[1] The separability of the objectives depends largely on the separability of the technologies, a point that we take up later, when we address technology as a source of complexity.

[2] For a fuller discussion of nested objectives, see Appendix B.

to disable an adversary, or they might factor into meeting an ultimate objective differently or, perhaps, interactively. If all the objectives were not equally important or contributed differently, we could employ weights (e.g., price- or preference-based) or a trading scheme to group them as if they were one or to choose among them, but that too would add heft to the analysis and, potentially, would require additional data or professional judgment.[3]

Fluid or Hard-to-Measure Objectives

When we say that an objective is *fluid*, we mean that it violates one or more of the conditions of fixity—wherein *fixity* refers to the extent to which an objective is known, bounded, and unchanging—and when we say that an objective is hard to measure, we mean that we cannot gauge it accurately or reliably for those or other reasons. Figure 3.2 illustrates this premise.

Contextual variation, risk, and uncertainty, which we address below, can contribute to the implausibility of a truly known, bounded, and unchanging objective. For example, in a dynamic operating environment, the objective could change, expand, or be revealed over time, depending partly on how an adversary responds. That said, we can try to work around the fluidity by specifying a possible fixed and measurable objective (denoted by level, amount, intensity, time frame, etc.) and then experimenting with deviations from the specification to identity a relatively robust solution. However, doing so would require not just imagination and computing power but also additional data, assumptions, and professional judgment.

Constraints on Attaining Objectives

Lastly, we consider the possibility of various constraints on attaining objectives, regardless of the objectives' singularity, fixity, or amenability to measurement. In some situations, it might be necessary to impose a constraint on the objective, such as achieving something in a specific amount, meaning neither less than nor more than that amount. In some instances, attaining *too little* of something would mean failing entirely and attaining *too much* of an objective could be counterproductive. Here, we might imagine examples involving damages

FIGURE 3.2
Violations of Fixity

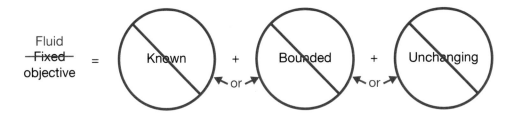

---

[3] Depending on how we represented the objectives and the weights or rules for trading among the objectives, we could be suggesting that some objectives are not truly fixed as "must-haves." For example, if we allowed some objectives to be traded for others, then some might fall away entirely. For suggested readings on this topic that include concrete examples and an introduction to multiobjective decisionmaking, see Appendix B.

that must be sufficient to render a target inoperable or halt an adversary but not so severe as to lead to escalation or trigger a draconian response. Similarly, if time is a factor, it might be necessary to meet the objective in a particular moment or within a specific interval. For example, if resources are being allocated to meet a series of sequential objectives, because targets must be destroyed in a certain order to have a disabling effect, it might be necessary to eliminate the first target quickly enough to reapply the resources to eliminate the next target before the adversary has time to regroup and stop the progression.

Such constraints serve to limit the alternatives for technologies and paths because any technologies or paths under consideration must be able to satisfy them. In the foregoing example of time-delineated sequential objectives, the speed of execution would constitute a feasibility constraint on the technologies and paths. In addition, we might also encounter more-direct constraints along the paths; for example, some forms of collateral damage or unintended consequences may be impermissible, regardless of the objectives.

Admittedly, not all constraints on objectives or technologies and paths imply greater complexity—sometimes, limiting the range of the possible can, to the contrary, impart simplicity, by eliminating paths from consideration—but they can create analytical challenges and, when precision matters, increase the need for granularity.

Ancillary Benefits and Unintended Consequences

In our analyses, we define *ancillary benefits* and *unintended consequences* as additional good or bad results, respectively, that emerge from efforts to meet an objective but that are not part of the objective.[4] Arguably, these *spillovers* are equivalent to additional products or byproducts of the technologies or effects under consideration, but, regardless of the label, they must be factored into the analysis because they are not already embodied in the objective.[5]

If a technology produces effects that are more than necessary to meet the objective, we could consider treating the excess as an ancillary benefit—or, if harmful, an unintended consequence—but, if we are not sure about the extent of the need, we might represent the excess as excess per se. The excess could serve as a cushion against the potential for a shortfall and be treated as presenting an *option* with which to meet emerging needs.[6]

---

[4] For more details on our definition, see Chapter 2 and Appendix A, and for a more complete discussion of ancillary benefits and unintended consequences, as well as a figure that depicts them along a path to an objective, see Appendix B. As we noted in Chapter 2, unintended consequences could be positive or negative, but we follow a common practice in the literature and use the term to refer just to negative consequences.

[5] To value the spillovers, one would need to apply consistent designation rules; for example, ancillary benefits could be converted to objective-equivalent units or framed as cost offsets, but they must be treated the same way in the analysis of each alternative. OMB (2003, p. 12) discusses some of the implications of ancillary benefits for conducting a CEA and how to address them, which we include in a note in Appendix B.

[6] We discuss real options in Appendix C. In broad terms, "[a]n option offers the right, but not the obligation to take specific future actions depending on how uncertain future conditions evolve" (Diana I. Angelis, David Ford, and John Dillard, "Real Options in Military Acquisition: A Retrospective Case Study of the

Lastly, there could be some instances in which a result can be construed as either an ancillary benefit or an additional objective, depending on the importance of the result to leadership. In this case, the underlying reality does not change—i.e., the technology produces what it produces—but how we think about the result changes. The result might be seen as either an "extra" or a "must-have," depending on leadership's perspective. If, for example, a technology is fast enough both to meet a stated objective, such as disabling an adversary, and to eliminate another target that leadership deems valuable but nonessential, then the opportunity to eliminate that target would constitute an ancillary benefit. If, instead, leadership deems the target essential, we could frame eliminating it as a second objective. Similarly, achieving an objective more quickly could be described as a "nice-to-have" or be integrated into the requirement for meeting the objective. Stated somewhat more colloquially, the difference between an ancillary benefit and an objective might be in the eye of the beholder. So long as an additional result constitutes *just* an ancillary benefit, the difficulty of the analysis increases *only* by as much as the difficulty of factoring the result into a bottom line; however, once the result is elevated to an objective, the analysis must include a path to meeting it.

Technology

Technology, like objectives, can impart complexity that presents varying degrees of analytical difficulty. A weapon system might have utility across many and varied use cases, it might serve its purpose alone or with other weapon systems, and different features of the systems might present a higher or lower priority in each case.

The versatility of a weapon system can manifest in at least two ways:

- A system might be capable of delivering more than one service at different times or in different situations, which we refer to as *flexibility*.
- A system might be capable of delivering more than one service at the same time or in the same situation, which we refer to as *jointness*.

For example, a weapon system that exhibits flexibility could be used to destroy one target in one engagement and another target in another engagement—but just one target *or* another target in the same engagement—whereas a system that exhibits jointness could be used to destroy both targets—one target *and* another target—in the same engagement.

Versatility itself can be a desirable characteristic, especially in view of risk or uncertainty,[7] but the potential to use a technology to jointly achieve multiple effects or objectives might require a more holistic view of the choice among alternatives. Specifically, one might need to

---

Javelin Anti-Tank Missile System," in Francois Melese, Anke Richter, and Binyam Solomom, eds., *Military Cost-Benefit Analysis: Theory and Practice*, Routledge, 2015, p. 349, citing Brealey and Meyers, 2000). Like Angelis, Ford, and Dillard (2015), we are concerned in this report with *real options*, which involve tangible assets.

[7] We discuss the value of versatility in terms of real options in Appendix C.

compare the costs of using technologies, either separately or in combinations, to elicit all the relevant effects or meet all the relevant objectives, collectively, as a package.[8] Looking instead at the costs of the alternatives in relation to each effect or objective separately could be misleading. For example, if faced with a set of two objectives such that all the technologies that can meet the second objective can also meet the first, then any technology that can meet only the first would be superfluous, regardless of its relative cost.

Complementarities among technologies can also create entanglements that impart complexity. For example, if weapon systems across technologies must be used together to meet an objective, their dependency would bear on both the analysis of the path from the technologies to the objective and the cost calculations along that path. Regarding the latter, it might suggest, as we discuss below, casting a wider net in cost estimation (e.g., to include not just costs that are specific to a primary weapon system but also costs of supporting systems).

Lastly, different features of the systems (e.g., payload, range, maneuverability, stealth, recoverability) can present higher or lower priorities in different use cases, but it might be hard to relate the costs of these features to their benefits when the operating environment is subject to change. The need for or utility of different features of a weapon system can emerge over time and emerge differently in different situations so that the full variety of use cases and, hence, objectives, might be unknowable at the outset. Moreover, we might know more about one weapon system than another, including the suitability of each in different operating environments. For example, one technology might be well-established and battlefield-proven, a second technology might be fully developed but not yet battlefield-proven, and a third technology might still be under development.

Context

For our purposes, *context* consists of all the behavioral (e.g., strategic or nonstrategic) and nonbehavioral (e.g., physical, spatial, temporal, or other environmental) characteristics that define a particular situation or describe the state of the world. In effect, context is everything about the problem space that we do not cover elsewhere in this section, implying a multitude of channels for complexity and, relatedly, suggesting the commensurate need for potentially wide-ranging assumptions that could grow with scope and realism. In simulations, we would capture context when we set values for the parameters of the model that correspond to the various behavioral and nonbehavioral characteristics of the operating environment. We might need to assume many of those values in the absence of supporting data and good foresight, which also relates to the prevalence of risk and uncertainty.

---

[8] In this case, the denominator in the calculation would be the set of all the effects or objectives, not just a single effect or objective. Appendix B provides a fuller discussion of the implications of flexible and joint technologies for decisionmaking in relation to multiple, potentially risky or uncertain objectives.

Boundaries

Boundaries, perhaps more than other sources of complexity, are not just about homing in on the nature of an underlying reality or even how realistically to depict it but also about choosing the question. Recall from Chapter 2 that "[c]osts and benefits do not exist—they are not defined—until the case is designed,"[9] but to design a case—or, in our approach, a CEA—we must decide where to draw a circle around the problem space.[10] The bigger the circle and the more we include in the problem space, the more complexity we might expect to encounter, almost by definition.

Decisions about boundaries require professional judgment because there might be no right answer, even with a singular, fixed, and measurable objective. For example, we might ask how wide to cast the net on costs (e.g., to include or exclude different types of direct costs—such as unit or life-cycle, per operation, per theater—indirect costs, other systems' support costs, and other services' costs) and over what time horizon. Relatedly, we might limit an analysis to a technology's primary effects or cast a wider net to include its secondary, tertiary, or nth order effects and their ancillary benefits or unintended consequences.[11] Although the act of drawing a circle around the problem space might naturally affect the realism of an analysis, we can still choose to make an analysis more or less realistic for any given circle. We return to this theme, with a specific application to cost estimation, in the section on realism.

Risk and Uncertainty

We conclude this section with a short discussion of risk and uncertainty and how it can add complexity to the analysis through any of the aforementioned channels but, perhaps most importantly, in relation to objectives and the context in which they occur. In this report, we draw a distinction between risk and uncertainty:

- *Risk* refers to the potential for multiple outcomes that are knowable and for which likelihood is measurable (e.g., as a matter of probability and severity, in common military usage, or mean and variance, in economic analysis).
- *Uncertainty* refers to the potential for multiple outcomes that are either unknowable or, even if knowable, for which likelihood is not measurable.[12]

---

[9] Schmidt, 2002, p. 5.

[10] Although we refer to *a circle*, this is not just a matter of drawing one circle but rather drawing a set of circles for different aspects of the problem space. For a related discussion of boundaries and approaches to setting them, see Victoria A. Greenfield and Letizia Paoli, *Assessing the Harms of Crime: A New Framework for Criminal Policy*, Oxford University Press, 2022, pp. 241–244.

[11] See Greenfield and Paoli (2022, pp. 77–78) for a discussion of infinitude.

[12] For a short note on the distinction between risk and uncertainty, see Robert S. Pindyck and Daniel L. Rubinfeld, *Microeconomics*, 9th ed., Pearson, 2018, p. 180, which cites economist Frank Knight's seminal work from the 1920s (Frank Knight, *Risk, Uncertainty, and Profit*, Houghton Mifflin Company, 1921). For Knight (1921), who was refuting the assumption of "practical omniscience" (p. 197) in economic analysis,

We can assign parameters to the former, but not readily to the latter.

This report tends to address risk more often than uncertainty, but, even if we can parametrize risk, a lack of perfect foresight can add complexity to the problem space and require us to consider a broad variety of possible objectives, contexts, or costs.[13] In our discussion of sequential or nested objectives, we found that choosing among alternative paths need not be daunting so long as we know where we need to go and can trace the paths to getting there. However, if these conditions do not hold—that is, if we can speculate only as to the objective or the paths from technologies to the objective—the analysis could falter. Much of the challenge of the analysis comes down to fixity, but the longer the path and the further we must project it, the less certainty we might have about the points along the path, let alone the endpoint. The length of a path from technologies to objectives—and, relatedly, the extent of uncertainty—might also depend on the form of the resource allocation decision. For example, if we are conducting an economic analysis for a purchase decision in which a weapon system could serve many purposes, some of which might yet be undiscovered, both the objectives and context could be uncertain. Alternatively, if we already own a weapon system and are deciding how to use it in an ongoing engagement, we might be able to quantify the range of the possible. We might also, as we suggest in Figure 3.1, anticipate more speculation as we move from engagement to battlefield to campaign, as evident in the greater relevance of professional judgment.

Inserting Realism into the Analysis

Producing a realistic analysis means depicting the problem space as it is—with whatever complexity it entails, at whatever level it occurs—but inserting realism in an analysis can also

---

the key distinction was one of being able to measure a condition's likelihood—he refers to a quantity that is "susceptible of measurement" (pp. 19–20)—but to be able to measure a condition's likelihood, the condition, itself, must also be known or at least knowable. Knight reserves the term *risk* for "measurable uncertainty" and the term *uncertainty* for unmeasurable uncertainty (p. 233), and he explores the practical difference between them. In Knight's own words (1921, p. 233),

> [t]he practical difference between the two categories, risk and uncertainty, is that in the former the distribution of the outcome in a group of instances is known (either through calculation a priori or from statistics of past experience), while in the case of uncertainty this is not true, the reason being in general that it is impossible to form a group of instances, because the situation dealt with is in a high degree unique. The best example of uncertainty is in connection with the exercise of judgment or the formation of those opinions as to the future course of events, which opinions (and not scientific knowledge) actually guide most of our conduct.

We, drawing from the economics and finance literature, use the term *outcomes* broadly to cover a variety of possible results, consequences, or instances, including the selling price of a stock, whether a coin lands on heads or tails, or, for our purposes, whether a missile destroys its intended target. For more on these definitions, see Appendix B; Pindyck and Rubinfeld, 2018; and Knight, 1921.

[13] In Appendix C, we show how to account for the value of flexibility when we lack information about the future at different points in a decisionmaking process.

make it more difficult. Producing a realistic representation of the problem space can be difficult for reasons related to technical model development and the need for assumptions and professional judgment. Furthermore, producing a realistic representation can increase the difficulty of applying the model to perform the analysis by increasing the need for computing power and data, neither of which might be readily available. In this section, we discuss how we can insert realism into the analysis, both in depicting paths from technologies to objectives and by making different decisions in cost estimation. We also show how complexity and realism can interact by tying the discussion back to boundaries.

Depicting Paths from Technologies to Objectives

Models are, by necessity, simplifications of the real world. However, to be useful, models must contain sufficient detail to capture the salient features of the problem space. Even models designed to inform relatively simple questions, such as a question of technology choice for a single engagement, require substantial investment in model development, data collection, assumptions, and professional judgment. Examples of such assumptions include treating complex weapon systems consisting of multiple vehicles as single immovable points in space, abstracting realities of aircraft basing and crewing to a fixed number of hours of aircraft flight times and downtimes, and assuming that the platform and munitions effectiveness in a real-world environment can be represented by average probabilities of kill (p_ks). Generating a model depiction—with these and many other simplifying assumptions—might still require many lines of code. Relaxing the assumption for the sake of adding realism to the depiction means even more code, more data requirements, more assumptions, and more professional judgment, further increasing the difficulty of modeling the problem. At a given level of analysis—such as engagement, battlefield, or campaign, which is correlated with complexity as discussed in the previous section—increased realism tends to increase modeling difficulty.

Calculating Costs

Computing costs realistically in an economic analysis can be difficult for several reasons. The difficulty of including specific cost components might stem from challenges in finding data, applying available data, or, as also relates to complexity, establishing boundaries on the cost estimation problem. Clearly defining the question at hand, such as whether we are considering a technology choice for an initial acquisition decision or a current employment decision, can affect decisions on how to draw these bounds. Challenges that stem from data availability and application can grow with realism primarily because more realism is likely to require more data, which, in turn, might contain more embedded assumptions. In modeling terms, a parameter value might not be a fact but rather an amalgam of fact and professional judgment.

We might also find that adding more realism can raise problems of insufficient data resolution or misalignment. That is, we might want to attribute costs in greater detail than the data can support because the data have not been collected at that level of detail or by the needed type of detail. For example, we might want to consider three subcategories of a cost, but available data sources might not provide the needed breakdown. It is not that the data are not good but that the data are collected for purposes that do not map to our purpose.

Similar data-related complications can arise when we draw increasingly large circles around costs (e.g., to attribute acquisition and life-cycle costs or costs of peripherals and dependencies that move beyond operations and sustainment [O&S] and toward the supporting units and infrastructure for the mission and overall campaign). Here, we see the interrelatedness of complexity and realism; when we add to the complexity of the problem space by extending the boundaries, we also make it more challenging to add realism. Drawing a larger circle around a larger problem means that we have more to handle in the estimation process.

Summary Observations on Complexity and Realism

In this section, we conclude our discussion of complexity and realism with summary observations, including on the difficulty of dealing with complexity and realism in a CEA compared with a CBA or BCA.

In the previous two sections, we reviewed some of the main challenges to generalizing CEA, which we group broadly as *complexity* and *realism*. The first category refers to the nature of the problem space and the second category refers to our depiction of it. One might say that the difference is in the balance of "determinism" and "free will." Within the first category, complexity, we pointed to the relevance of the level of analysis—be it an engagement, the battlefield, or a campaign—as both a source of complexity and a driver of other sources of complexity. We noted that the level of analysis can, for example, bear on the form of the objective and the extent of risk or uncertainty in the operating environment. Although interconnectedness among different sources of complexity makes it hard to single out one source as more important than the rest, fixity—or its lack—stands paramount among them, along with the potential for risk and uncertainty that can undermine fixity and interact with the other sources of complexity, especially context. At risk of repetition, it helps to know where you are going. Regarding realism, we considered the limits of analytical feasibility, in relation to computing power and data availability, and how adding complexity, as in the case of cost estimation, can make it harder to increase realism.

We also discussed how increasing complexity and realism could entail greater reliance on assumptions—and, by extension, professional judgment—but noted that our concerns about relying on either would depend on the extent to which they sway the findings. When an assumption matters so much to a modeling effort that changing it would affect the resource allocation decision, we care more about it. More formally, we could say that we must regard the sensitivity of our findings to changes in our assumptions.

We conclude this section by considering how concerns about complexity or realism might differ for other forms of economic analysis, specifically, CBA and BCA. In a comparison that starts with our definitions of each method (see Chapter 2), the differences would manifest largely in the realm of objectives, albeit with reinforcement from related concerns about risk and uncertainty. The CEA might be said to be more needful of—or at least more inclined to benefit from—a hard and fast objective than either the CBA or BCA. The notion of fixity is especially important in a CEA because all costs must be assessed in relation to the objective and, perhaps even more so, for developing a CPO metric because the objective is the denominator. The distillation of an economic analysis to a point estimate that normalizes on the objective necessitates greater clarity regarding the objective because the objective anchors the calculation. A CBA might allow more leeway to consider broader circumstances, including comparisons across different kinds of objectives, and a BCA could account for more variables, although both a CBA and BCA could entail other challenges, relating to additional analytical and data requirements. One might imagine that, in the face of greater complexity or realism, it could be harder to value benefits or apply other technique to parameterize them.

CHAPTER 4

Battlefield-Level Cost-per-Objective

In this chapter, we describe a notional battlefield-level example of a technology choice and discuss the application of CEA to that example—as well as some of the potential challenges of conducting the CEA—using the theory presented in Chapter 3. More specifically, we explore using a CEA for selecting among technologies for achieving a distance strike against an enemy target in a notional future conflict.[1] We refer to this goal as the strike objective. The intent is to revisit the theory discussed in the previous chapters using a more concrete example, although we do so qualitatively because of the sensitive nature of relevant quantitative data inputs. A strike mission provides a timely and practical example because (1) it is relevant to existing decision points related to long-range fires within the services and DoD and (2) at least some planning factors and other data were available to conduct quantitative modeling from which we could draw insight, even though we could not present the modeling in this report.

In the rest of this chapter, we introduce the example related to the strike technology choice, show how to frame this example in the language of CEA, and use the example for a more concrete discussion of issues of complexity and realism. Lastly, we comment on the transferability of the theoretical framework to other kinds of decisions.

The Strike Example

Figure 4.1 provides a stylized representation of the strike example that we use throughout this chapter.[2] The three rows of Figure 4.1 represent three possible friendly (Blue) *technologies* that could achieve the strike objective but that each rely either more or less heavily on air- or ground-based assets. The technologies consist of *activities* that together *produce* specific *effects*. The Blue shooters fire at a predefined number of enemy (Red) targets to destroy them.

---

[1] Additional detail on this example is available in a companion report (Katharina Ley Best, Victoria A. Greenfield, Craig A. Bond, Nathaniel Edenfield, Mark Hvizda, John C. Jackson, Duncan Long, Jordan Willcox, *Beyond Cost-per-Shot: Illustrating the Use of Economic Analysis and Metrics in Defense Decisionmaking*, 2023, Not available to the general public). This section does not include results based on those details or related simulation modeling.

[2] For fuller definitions of these terms, see Appendix A.

FIGURE 4.1

Technology Alternatives and Associated Costs for a Strike Mission

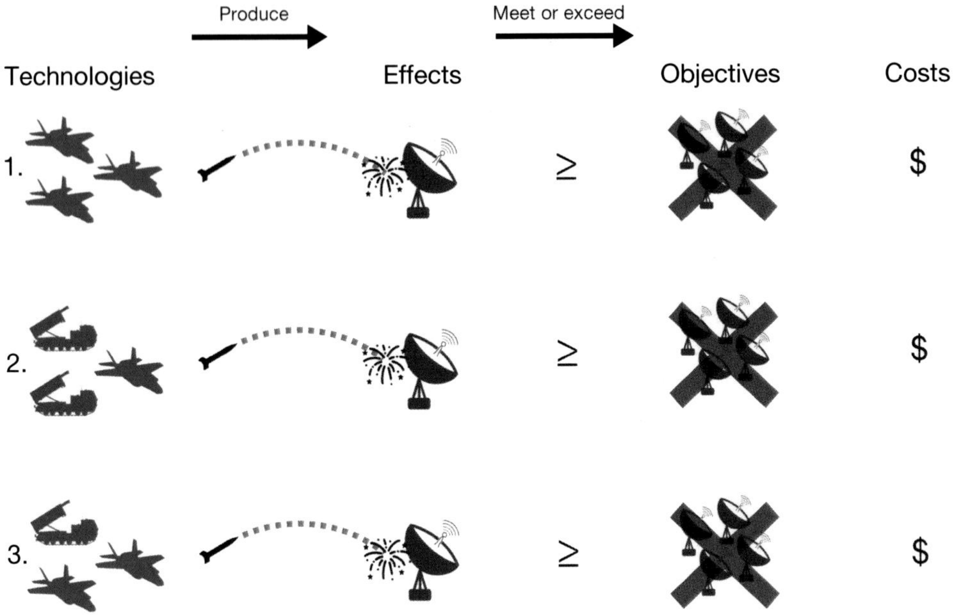

NOTE: Icons are intended to generally represent employment of a particular platform rather than provide specific counts. Aircraft icons represent air patrols, launcher icons represent ground-based launchers, red radar icons represent targets (with gray Xs representing the objective of destroying the targets), and munition icons represent needed munitions for this engagement. Technology 1 relies most heavily—indeed, solely—on air-based assets, Technology 2 relies least heavily on air-based assets, and Technology 3 represents a middling case. The dollar symbols in the final column represent costs that differ by technology.

The set of cumulative effects achieved by a technology are then measured against a desired *objective* to determine whether the overall strike mission has been achieved. Achieving the objective, via the activities, has an associated cost (measured in dollars) for each technology. In this chapter, we do not assume a single question to be answered by the analysis (such as "Which technology should DoD invest in?") but rather illustrate how slightly different assumptions might be appropriate depending on whether an economic analysis is intended to support a purchase question, an employment question, or some other type of technology choice.

The left-hand portion of Figure 4.1 is essentially analogous to Figure 2.1, in which we explored achieving a single effect: specifically, the destruction of a single target. In the strike example, we explore achieving multiple effects that, together, would achieve a single objective. We define success in terms of the ability to complete the strike mission as a binary condition; that is, the technology either can or cannot succeed. To achieve success, a technology must be able to destroy or disable all individual targets (effects), resulting in the completion of the strike mission (objective). Because success is defined in relation to the ability to achieve an objective rather than a singular effect, the metrics derived for analysis of this example are the result of cost-per-*objective* calculations rather than cost-per-*effect* calculations, and we use

CPO language throughout this chapter. Notwithstanding the ratio-like vocabulary of CPO, our specification of the problem, including a fixed objective, enables us to seek a relatively simple cost-minimizing solution.

Technology of the Strike Example

The three technologies in our example are designed to explore various levels of inclusion of ground-based fires—in addition to the default option of air-launched fires—for strike. The technologies consist of two bookend technologies that rely most and least heavily on air-based assets compared with land-based assets (Technologies 1 and 2, respectively) and a representative technology somewhere in between them (Technology 3), which we call an *interior* technology. The technologies differ not just by the mix of weapon systems but also, consequently, by speed in terms of the time needed to achieve the strike objective, which we summarize as follows:

- **Technology 1 (*Air Only*)** relies solely on air-based assets to meet the objective (X). It will produce effects ≥ X to meet the objective, but it will meet the objective more slowly than a technology that uses both air- and ground-based fires, such as Technology 2.
- **Technology 2 (*Air + Ground with ISR*)** uses a mix of air and ground-based assets. Specifically, it employs the maximum number of ground-based shooters, based on availability, and augments them with the fewest possible air-based shooters required to meet the objective. It will also produce effects ≥ X to meet the objective (X), but it will meet the objective more rapidly than a technology that uses only aircraft, such as Technology 1.
- **Technology 3 (*Air + Ground without ISR*)** uses a mix of air- and ground-based assets that is somewhere between Technologies 1 and 2, such that its speed of meeting the objective (X) is also between the speeds of those two technologies.

As indicated by the technology names, the difference between the maximal and middling cases hinges on the difference in the capabilities of the ground-based assets and whether those capabilities include intelligence, surveillance, and reconnaissance (ISR), or sensing. In the maximal case, ground units can provide their own ISR and can perform targeting and execute missions even when sensing aircraft are unavailable or exhausted, as might happen during the later phases of an operation. In the middling case, ground units cannot provide their own ISR, and, although they can strike in place of air-based assets, air-based assets must continue to serve in the sensing role. Thus, the maximal case relies less heavily on air-based assets than the middling case, which relies less heavily on air-based assets than the air-only case. A visual representation of the three technologies is presented in Figure 4.2, adding additional detail to the depiction in Figure 4.1.

FIGURE 4.2
Strike Technology Alternatives

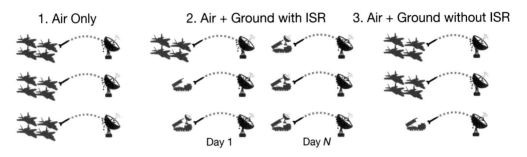

NOTE: Icons are intended to generally represent the employment of a particular platform rather than provide specific counts. The cluster of four aircraft icons represents an air patrol, the launcher icon represents a set of launchers required to engage a single target (with the small blue radar icon indicating the use of ground-based targeting), the red radar icons represent single targets, and the munition icons represent the needed munitions for this engagement. The Technology 2 (Air + Ground with ISR) panel indicates that ground-based fires can locate targets both based on aircraft-provided targeting and via native targeting capability, with the ability to use native targeting capability potentially being most useful in later parts of the mission when air assets are unavailable or otherwise employed.

In all three technologies, in a single period, a single Red target can be eliminated using air-based assets when they are available, with additional Red targets potentially being eliminated using ground-based assets in Technologies 2 and 3. The availability of air-based assets is a limiting factor in terms of shooter capacity in all three technologies, but having loitering aircraft in the air is a hard requirement for only Technologies 1 and 3, in which ground-based shooters do not have sensing capabilities. In Technologies 2 and 3, the availability of ground-based assets with suitable capabilities is also a limiting factor. Although the specifics of how these technologies conduct strike is outside the scope of this report, we lay out a few assumptions here so that we can use them in the examples in the rest of this chapter. We assume that the performance of the *Air Only* technology alternative is constrained by the availability of aircraft for deployment of a strike package, their presence (loiter) in the battlespace (aircraft must be flying to shoot at a target, and each strike package of aircraft can engage only one target), and the emission of (or other detectable activity by) Red targets during that loiter period (Red targets can be detected only if they are emitting). The *Air + Ground with ISR* technology alternative is constrained by the availability of ground-based launchers and, to some extent, the rate of emission by Red targets; ground-based fires can shoot any time, but they will have good information on target location only when Red targets have recently emitted. The *Air + Ground without ISR* technology alternative is again constrained by aircraft availability and loiters (because the aircraft provide targeting), as well as the emission of Red targets during the loiter period. Additionally, this technology is constrained by the availability of ground-based launchers. The limitations of each technology are notionally depicted in Figure 4.3.

FIGURE 4.3

Assumed Limiting Factors Across Technologies

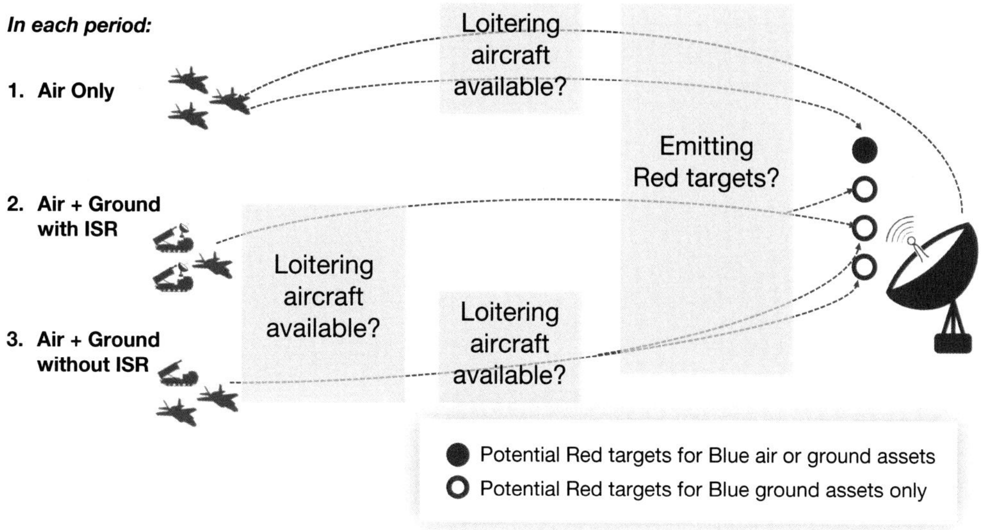

NOTE: Icons are intended to generally represent the employment of a particular platform rather than provide specific counts. Blue air packages are assumed to be effective against one emitting surface-to-air missile (SAM) (filled red circle), whereas the number of Red SAMs that can be targeted by ground assets depends on the p_k of ground-based fires (open red circles). The small blue radar icons indicate the use of ground-based targeting.

Applying CEA to Compare Technology Alternatives for Strike

In Table 4.1, we show how we frame the question of technology choice for our strike example in the language of a CEA. In effect, we restate the resource allocation decision in Figure 4.1 by specifying the characteristics of the technologies under consideration, the objective, and the necessary effects, along with their potential costs, ancillary benefits, and unintended consequences. This allocation decision centers on choosing among different combinations of two weapon systems (one is air-based, the other ground-based) that can strike to achieve a fixed numerical objective (X) measured in terms of Red target kills. The use of each system is the activity, the combination of systems is the technology, and the associated strikes are the effect (which must be ≥ X, which is the objective in terms of the number of kills). By referring to the combinations of the weapon systems as *technologies*, we imply that different allocations of the systems constitute different technologies.

The speed of the mission, which is inherent to the asset mix, in turn affects the accrual of costs, ancillary benefits, and unintended consequences. Although the types of costs, ancillary benefits, and unintended consequences can be the same for each technology, the amounts of each, like the amount of the effect (≥ X), can differ.[3] Costs accrue from execution, Blue asset

---

[3] The technologies might yield different amounts of effects, costs, ancillary benefits, or unintended consequences, even if they can all produce enough effects (≥ X) to meet the objective.

TABLE 4.1

Strike Technology Alternatives in the Language of Cost-Effectiveness Analysis

Attribute	Technology 1	Technology 2	Technology 3
Description	• Single platform (*Air Only*) • Air > minimum, ground = 0 • Slower	• Mixed platform (*Air + Ground with ISR*) (ground maximum) • Air = minimum, ground = maximum • Faster	• Mixed platform (*Air + Ground without ISR*) • Air > minimum, ground < maximum • Intermediate
Objective (fixed, measurable)	• Red target kills = X	• Red target kills = X	• Red target kills = X
Effects	• Strikes $\geq$ X[a]	• Strikes $\geq$ X	• Strikes $\geq$ X
Costs	• Execution (e.g., munitions) • Attrition (air, ground) • Rent[b]	• Execution (e.g., munitions) • Attrition (air, ground) • Rent	• Execution (e.g., munitions) • Attrition (air, ground) • Rent
Ancillary benefits	• Less Blue ground attrition = 0 • Time savings = 0 • Unique activity option = 0	• Less Blue ground attrition $\geq$ 0 • Time savings $\geq$ 0 • Unique activity option $\geq$ 0	• Less Blue ground attrition $\geq$ 0 • Time savings $\geq$ 0 • Unique activity option $\geq$ 0
Unintended consequences	• More Blue other attrition • Casualties	• More Blue other attrition • Casualties	• More Blue other attrition • Casualties

NOTE: We refer to air-based assets and ground-based assets as *air* and *ground*, respectively.

[a] We assume that it is not possible to "kill" *x* Red targets with fewer than *x* strikes.

[b] *Rent* is an implicit rate based on the marginal value of next-best use other than in the strike mission.

attrition, and rent, in which *rent* is an implicit rate based on the marginal value of next-best use other than in the strike mission. For example, the same aircraft that would be used for the strike mission might be usable for conducing some other activity—which also holds value—if the aircraft were not already being used for the strike mission. Ancillary benefits can take the form, for example, of reduced Blue ground attrition, time saving (which might have value apart from its direct effects on costs), or the ability to execute a technology-specific unique activity of some kind. Unintended consequences could include higher attrition of Blue ground forces (outside the assets directly involved in the strike mission) and casualties. In some instances, we may set the value of a cost, benefit, or consequence to zero, as in the case of the unique activity option, which we specify as pertaining only to technologies that employ some land power.[4]

In this chapter, we do not discuss how to solve for the optimal mix of systems. Instead, we discuss how to assess the relative costs, ancillary benefits, and unintended consequences of the proposed bookend technologies and a representative interior technology. In theory, we

---

[4] As noted previously, this need not be the case.

could find the optimal mix by assessing the costs, benefits, and attributes of all the feasible technologies—including the bookends and everything in between—and selecting the lowest-cost technology among them.

In the rest of this chapter, we use this framing to explore some of the sources of complexity and effects of realism that we discussed abstractly in Chapter 3. Specifically, we provide a more concrete treatment of the effects of a potentially multifaceted or fluid objective, the effects of contextual variation, and the effects of making different assumptions and decisions about what to include and with how much detail in cost estimation.

Sources of Complexity in the Strike Example

In this section, we apply our typology of sources of complexity (Box 3.1) to our notional strike example—and introduce modest variations—to consider how complexity might arise and contribute to the difficulty of conducting an economic analysis, including a CEA for the strike example. We do not address risk and uncertainty separately because these concepts enter much of the discussions of each of the other sources of complexity, either implicitly or explicitly. As suggested in Chapter 3, some sources of complexity, especially those pertaining to the objective, can present greater challenges in a CEA—and the derivation of related metrics—than in a CBA or BCA, but they would still bear on the conduct of a BCA.

The Objective

As discussed in Chapter 3, a fixed objective is a central premise of a CEA and, consequently, any related metric derivations. Framing a real-world question in the form of whether it is possible to achieve a fixed objective requires making assumptions about how to define that objective, which will bear on the results of the analysis. In our notional strike example, we specified a single, fixed objective; however, we can elaborate on that example with modest variations to demonstrate the potential for complexity.

Multiple Objectives

The success or failure of a strike mission can be multidimensional, implying the potential for multiple objectives. For example, target strikes might need to be achieved quickly so that assets can be freed up to accomplish a related second objective. That second objective could be to attack targets in another geographical area (also a battlefield-level objective) or to finish operations in time to avoid violating a ceasefire or to respect a holiday (possibly a campaign-level objective). The latter could also be represented as a *constraint* on the time required to achieve the strike objective, as we discuss later in this chapter.

Multiple objectives can become more difficult to incorporate when they are sequential or interdependent, such as when multiple strike missions are underway at the same time and the ultimate objective is related to the cumulative outcome of those missions, in the aggregate, and not to a single fixed objective for each mission. For example, there might be multiple geographical areas that could be used as access corridors for aerial attacks deeper into enemy territory. In that case, strike missions must be executed in all geographic areas to ensure the enemy cannot ascertain which corridor Blue forces intend to use, but the full strike objective might need to be achieved only in one or a small number of geographic areas.

Fluid or Hard-to-Measure Objectives

Recall that a fluid objective is an objective that violates the properties of being known, bounded, and unchanging. The exemplary objective of disabling a known number of targets is not fluid, but it might not accurately reflect the realities of the battlefield. For example, a strike objective might not be *known* because Blue forces might not know how many Red targets are present or even whether achieving the strike mission is the right objective to focus on during this part of the overall campaign. Even if the number of targets is known, success could be hard to measure if available information on the result of a strike is imperfect. In that case, the exact amount of force required and even the state of progress toward meeting the objective are unknown. Information availability could also differ across the technologies, further increasing the difficulty of an economic analysis. A strike-related objective might not be well *bounded* if, for example, executing the mission uncovers new threats, requiring additional resources, which, in turn, uncover new threats, and so on, potentially without a clear endpoint. Finally, the strike-related objective could fail to be *unchanging* because Red forces can react to Blue action. Red targets might stop emitting, making them hard to find, or additional Red forces might threaten Blue air- or ground-based assets. At the campaign level, Red reactions could include decisions to escalate or end fighting or to make political moves instead of engaging on the battlefield. Figure 4.4 builds on Figure 3.2 to summarize some of these examples.

FIGURE 4.4
Possible Violations of Fixity in the Strike Example

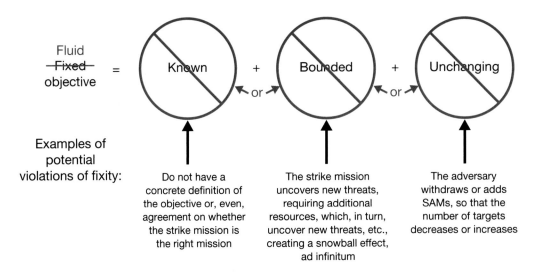

Constraints on Attaining Objectives

If time is a consideration in completing the strike mission then, as suggested previously, success could be defined with a constraint, as "disabling a fixed number of Red targets (X) within *N* hours." This objective adds a constraint to the original objective by appending a functional requirement in terms of the allowable time to complete the mission. It is possible that such an additional constraint could result in a different technology choice; for example, the most cost-effective technology alternative for destroying the fixed number of Red targets, based on its CPO metric, could be the slowest, and it might miss the timing requirement. Comparing the three technologies laid out at the beginning of this chapter, it might be the case that slower technologies, such as *Air Only* and possibly *Air + Ground without ISR*, cannot achieve the objective of eliminating the required number of Red targets within *N* hours, thus making *Air + Ground with ISR* the preferred technology, regardless of its cost. Other constraints, such as those on weapons usage, the stationing of ground-based launchers, detectability, or casualties could also be considered.

Ancillary Benefits and Unintended Consequences

Instead of changing the objective, an analysis can also consider valuing ancillary benefits or unintended consequences. As discussed in the previous chapter, ancillary benefits and unintended consequences are results that are valued in some manner—either positively or negatively—but that accrue *in addition to* the benefits and costs associated with achieving the objective. In cases in which these benefits or costs can be monetized, they can be used as a cost offset in the derivation of the CPO metric to compare alternative technologies on an apples-to-apples basis. However, which real-world ancillary benefits and unintended consequences to include and how to quantify them is generally up to the interpretation of the analyst.

Using the notional strike example, we present two types of ancillary benefits in Figure 4.5 that might be relevant to decisionmakers: one that can be monetized (left-hand side of Figure 4.5) and one that cannot (right-hand side of Figure 4.5). On the left-hand side of the figure, ancillary benefits related to executing an additional ground attack mission are translatable into impacts on Blue asset attrition, which is one of the cost drivers in our strike example. On the right-hand side of the figure, ancillary benefits related to time savings cannot directly be translated into dollars. It is also worth noting that the monetizable benefits on the left-hand side accrue during the strike mission and the non-monetizable benefits accrue after the strike mission. However, the temporal—*during* and *after*—distinction is not the source of the analytical difference in monetizability. Benefits could accrue during or after the mission and be more or less monetizable, depending on the form they take.

In the monetizable case on the left-hand side of Figure 4.5, we assume that the addition of ground-based fires frees up air assets to execute additional missions (e.g., ground attack) during the strike operation, which results, ultimately, in less Blue attrition overall. More specifically, it is possible that adding ground-based fires frees up air assets to perform additional

FIGURE 4.5
Selected Ancillary Benefits for Strike Example

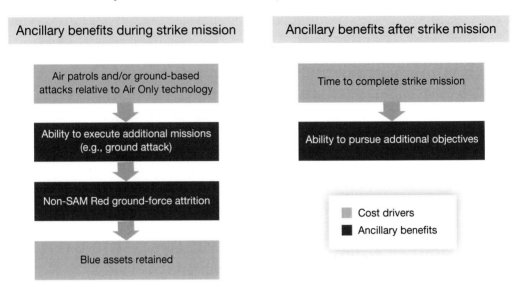

missions that degrade enemy forces, resulting in less attrition of Blue tanks and other techni-cal assets, some of which were not associated with the strike objective. The retention of these assets, the value of which can be monetized based on their purchase costs, are thus additional benefits to Blue forces that accrue outside the strike mission (hence *ancillary*) but are relevant to the overall warfighting effort. Given the potential for monetization, the additional benefits in the form of avoided costs relative to the *Air Only* reference case could be subtracted from the overall costs associated with the strike mission in the CPO metric.

In the non-monetizable case on the right-hand side of Figure 4.5, we assume that a shorter time to strike completion frees up assets that can then pursue additional objectives earlier than they could have been pursued otherwise. The *Air + Ground* technologies provide addi-tional assets for strike, thus potentially reducing the time required to succeed. Presumably, there is some benefit to completing the strike mission faster. Although the reduction in time to completing the strike mission might be quantifiable, it is not immediately clear how to monetize the value of the reduction. The lack of a straightforward approach to monetiza-tion means that the CPO metric cannot be adjusted to compare the analytical results con-sistently across the three technologies. Answering the technology choice question at a level that includes these ancillary benefits could require a reframing of the objective, possibly to encompass them as part of the objective.

Technology

The characterization of technologies in this chapter assumes that the three technologies—and the platforms and capabilities that compose them—have only a single purpose: specifi-cally, participation in strike. This characterization is, of course, a gross simplification because weapon systems have utility across multiple types of missions. The capabilities involved in our three technologies (aircraft, launchers, targets, and munitions, not to mention personnel, command and control resources, planning, sustainment, and logistics) could, as evident in the foregoing discussion of ancillary benefits, be used for other things. For example, aircraft are *flexible*—meaning they can deliver a different capability in a different situation—in that they could also be used to fly reconnaissance missions or participate in air-to-air combat at different points in time. The ISR capabilities on ground-based shooters could be *jointly* useful for two different missions if they are able to detect multiple kinds of targets simultaneously. An economic analysis that does not account for the value of versatility—in terms of both flexibility and jointness—might fail to capture some of the value of one technology or another. Appendix B provides additional detail on how such versatility can affect an economic analysis, and Appendix C discusses how framing versatility in terms of real options can help to capture that value.

Context

Even if a fixed objective provides a sufficiently realistic representation of the problem at hand, estimating what it takes to achieve the fixed objective can become more difficult if the context in which the objective must be achieved is not fully known or knowable. In this section, we explore the effects of risk and uncertainty in assumptions about the context on the ability to compute and apply a CPO metric. If battlefield conditions are unknown or potentially changing over time, the analysis might need to include an exploration of a large parameter space and assess the robustness of the CPO results to variations in Blue air attrition, Blue ground p_k, and Red operational tempo (OPTEMPO), as shown in Figure 4.6. Taken together with the details of cost drivers, plausible changes in the values of these parameters can have an effect large enough to change the rankings of CPOs across technologies and, hence, the conclusions of the economic analysis.

The primary cost drivers in our strike example are replacement platform costs of attrited platforms and munition costs. The specifics of the context in which the strike mission is undertaken can change the relative contribution of these factors and can affect each of the technologies differently. For example, because aircraft are generally very expensive assets, assumptions around aircraft attrition are potentially big drivers of cost. It is possible that if the rate of aircraft attrition is high, the cost of technologies more heavily reliant on aerial assets might be much larger than when aircraft attrition is low. Variation in context parameters could exacerbate this driver of cost. For example, in the *Air Only* technology, if we assume that each aerial patrol can engage only a single Red target, multiple Red targets emitting per period is likely to result in missed opportunities to fire on emitting targets and in increased likelihood of aircraft being destroyed. The cost of Blue aircraft attrition might dwarf the cost of ground-based munitions used by other technologies even if the ground-based munitions are more expensive than aerial ones.

FIGURE 4.6

Adding Contextual Variation to the Strike Model

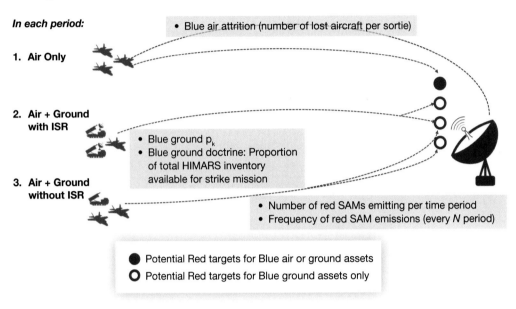

In each period:

• Blue air attrition (number of lost aircraft per sortie)

1. **Air Only**

2. **Air + Ground with ISR**

• Blue ground p_k
• Blue ground doctrine: Proportion of total HIMARS inventory available for strike mission

3. **Air + Ground without ISR**

• Number of red SAMs emitting per time period
• Frequency of red SAM emissions (every *N* period)

● Potential Red targets for Blue air or ground assets
○ Potential Red targets for Blue ground assets only

NOTE: Icons are intended to generally represent employment of a particular platform rather than provide specific counts. Blue air packages are assumed to be effective against one emitting SAM, whereas the number of Red SAMs that can be targeted by ground assets depends on the p_k of ground-based fires. The small blue radar icon indicates the use of ground-based targeting. HIMARS = High Mobility Artillery Rocket System.

On the other hand, when Blue aircraft attrition is relatively low, Blue ground missiles are relatively less effective, and only a small number of Red targets are available (emitting); the cost of ground-based munitions might be a more important driver of cost than aerial attrition. In such contexts, an *Air Only* technology might stand out as the least costly based on a comparison of CPO metrics across the technology alternatives.

Finally, some contexts might also be inopportune for technologies that are otherwise favored by a comparison of CPO metrics. For example, there could be many contexts in which the *Air + Ground with ISR* technology is the most cost-effective because it is the most capable: It provides the ability to strike multiple Red targets per period (even if the aerial patrol can strike only once) while also maximizing the use of ground-based fires (thus putting fewer expensive aircraft at risk). However, in cases in which the ground-based munition is expensive, the ground-based munition is less effective than the aerial munition, or successful hits from ground-based fires are more difficult to verify, the high employment of ground-based fires could lead to a high cost of employment for *Air + Ground with ISR*. This might be especially pronounced in contexts in which Red behavior leads to a large reliance on ground-based launchers (such as when many Red targets emit during each period, leaving all but the first to be engaged by ground-based assets).

Boundaries

The discussion in this chapter already touches on both the importance of bounding the problem space in an economic analysis, such as a CEA, and the roles that boundaries can play in determining not just the terms of the analysis but the results. The tighter the circle an analyst draws around the problem space, the more likely it is that other sources of complexity will lose relevance, but that will not change the underlying reality. If, for example, we assume the strike mission occurs in isolation and is independent of everything else going on in the campaign—so that we can focus our analytic attention on it and it alone—many of the foregoing complications related to such concerns as a fluid objective, the accrual of ancillary benefits, or the need to account for technological versatility could fall away. However, we must still decide whether defining the problem space this narrowly is appropriate, depending on the nature of the decision and what information policymakers can afford to lose in the comparison of technology alternatives. That is, can the results of the narrow analysis help to make the decision? We comment more specifically on boundaries related to cost estimation in the next section on realism and on related concerns about analytical feasibility and usefulness in the next chapter.

Realism in the Strike Example

In this section, we revisit the challenges of inserting realism into an economic analysis, also paralleling the themes from Chapter 3. As in that chapter, we focus on the paths from technologies to objectives and on cost estimation. We discuss how, for our strike example, inserting realism into an economic analysis might be analytically necessary—that is, it can affect the outcome of an analysis—even though doing so can increase the difficulty of the analysis. At a given level of analysis, including the battlefield level, increased realism tends to increase the difficulty of modeling and hence the analysis, but it might also be necessary for arriving at the *right* answer depending, as previously discussed, on the nature of the decision.

Depicting Paths from Technologies to Objectives

The paths from technologies to objectives can be depicted with more or less realism, as befits the analysis, but doing so can impart more or less difficulty. The least realistic representation of technology for the strike mission might assume overall attrition rates and munition expenditures for the whole strike mission without modeling any individual effects (e.g., a single shooter aiming at a single target). Such an exercise might be specified easily and require minimal data, computing power, or expert judgment, but it might only yield a ballpark-like answer to a broad resourcing question and, even then, could present risks if the broad brushstroke inadvertently misses a relevant parameter. A slightly more realistic model might depict individual effects, but it would do so in an abstract and simplified way based on planning factors. An increasingly realistic model—yet more difficult to specify, populate, and execute—could move beyond planning factors for average p_ks and attrition rates and instead represent additional realities of the battlefield explicitly. For example, a more realistic model might capture the details of the sensor-to-shooter loop and related airspace deconfliction for both ground- and air-based shooters or it might capture the physics of individual munitions and the individual components of the Red targets, allowing the model to delve into the very real technological differences in targeting ability and speed. Depending on the specifics of the analysis, the additional detail captured by the more realistic models might have a bearing on the outcome, including the rankings of the CPO metrics for each of the alternatives. For example, a small difference in the flight trajectory of one munition versus another could prove critical given the geography in which the strike mission takes place, meaning that reliance on CPO metrics that derive from a less realistic model could lead decisionmakers to the wrong technology choice.

Calculating Costs

Regardless of the cost implications of imparting more or less realism in the depiction of a technology, cost estimation can also be more or less realistic. As was true for depicting the paths from technologies to objectives, the decision about how much realism to insert in a cost estimate can bear on both the difficulty and outcome of an economic analysis.

Figure 4.7 gives a general representation of the potential components of a cost estimate for an economic analysis of our strike example, arrayed in an approximate hierarchy from most direct cost to more holistic, complete cost. The various cost components in Figure 4.7 also vary in terms of the difficulty of including them in a cost estimate, with difficulty sometimes (though not always) increasing as we move from direct to complete costs. Deciding which cost components to include is part of defining the level of realism of the cost estimate and is related to the question of setting boundaries for the economic analysis, as discussed earlier in this chapter. Once boundaries have been set, the difficulty of including the needed specific cost components might stem from challenges in finding data or applying available data. We discuss these three sources of realism-related challenges below.

Setting Boundaries on Cost Estimation

We first reconsider the problem of setting boundaries from the perspective of realism in cost estimation. To make an estimate more realistic, it might be necessary to draw a wider circle around the problem and include more—and more-detailed—information about costs, but doing so can make the analysis more difficult, in part, because it might require more expert judgment but also because it can raise some of the same challenges of data availability and attribution that we address below. For example, a more realistic cost estimate might include more of the costs associated with peripherals than a less realistic cost estimate, but those costs might be hard to tally, let alone attribute, in the analysis.

Depending on the question at hand, different decisions about which costs to include or exclude in an estimate—and at what level of detail—might be appropriate. In some applications, guidance may be available for or even dictate such decisions, but in other cases, the decision may rest largely with the analyst. In the case of a technology acquisition decision, it

44

FIGURE 4.7
Cost Components in Strike Cost Estimation

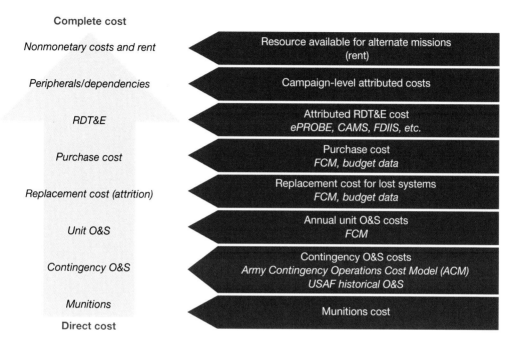

NOTE: CAMS = Capability and AROC [Army Requirements Oversight Council] Management System; ePROBE = e-Program Optimization and Budget Evaluation; FCM = FORCES Cost Model; FDIIS = Force Development Investment Information System; RDT&E = research, development, test, and evaluation. ACM and FCM are not available to the general public. For a brief description of these models, see Army Financial Management and Comptroller, "FORCES Information," webpage, Office of the Assistant Secretary of the Army, undated.

might be appropriate to include purchase costs fully, but in the case of a technology employment decision, an analyst might need to make assumptions about how much of the purchase cost can be attributed reasonably to the particular mission and whether a different attribution is appropriate if one platform has already been purchased and the other is being considered for acquisition. Depending on the differential between these purchase costs and other components of the cost estimate in Figure 4.7, these decisions might point to different technology choices. If replacement costs are a primary cost driver (as discussed in this strike example), then excluding replacement costs from the analysis would shrink the cost differences among the three technologies, and the higher aircraft attrition in the *Air Only* case would have no effect on cost.

Similarly, including the full life-cycle costs of a weapon system might be more obviously required for a technology acquisition decision than for a technology employment decision, but including the full life-cycle costs in the latter without further refinement could substantially alter the outcome of the analysis. In the confines of a single strike mission involving aircraft and launchers, acquisition and replacement costs would likely dwarf the O&S costs during the mission but not over the full life cycle of a weapon system.

Moreover, even within the confines of a single mission, an analyst must still decide how to bound O&S costs, some of which can be hard to capture. For example, analysts need to decide whether to consider costs associated with command and control units, combat service (e.g., engineering) and combat service support (e.g., resupply) units, or protection units (e.g., air defense), all of which make it possible for aircraft and launchers to function and could contribute to a more realistic depiction of costs. That brief list combines support necessary for the actual conduct of the mission and support necessary to put the platforms in the position to conduct the mission in the first place, suggesting that further refinement would require some parsing. However, no simple set of rules can be used to attribute assets and activities that have multiple—sometimes simultaneous—applications in a given theater to a single bounded mission. Even if the attribution of different types of activities were settled, cost estimation difficulties abound. The depth and breadth of supported and supporting relationships can shift within operations and change fundamentally in different theater circumstances.

These challenges compound as one considers expanding the circle still further. Even among the small set of platforms involved in our example, there are diverse cost considerations. The life-cycle costs of the hardware and the number and type of personnel who operate them are difficult to separate—and separate on equal terms—from the services that sustain them. Transparency is possible, but complete and fair treatment is very challenging. Decisions about how to include these kinds of costs could alter the outcome of the analysis because these costs might not accrue equally across technologies. Ground-based launchers, operating far forward, can be harder to supply. Aircraft, operating from a fixed location, can be harder to defend or can require unique logistics support. Omission represents a decision of unknown consequence, though again, we bear in mind that the preponderance of costs attributed to a given operation tend to lie in expended or attrited materiel.

Finding the Data

Once boundaries have been set and decisions have been made about which cost components to include, the analyst must find necessary data. Finding data for some aspects of the cost estimation problem can present greater challenges than for others, and data challenges are likely to grow as the boundaries expand and realism increases. Related to the strike example, finding data sources for the cost of expended munitions and attrited platforms is likely to be comparatively straightforward because manufacturers, governments, and other organizations publish that information. However, adding realism to account for fleet composition in a cost estimate—a fleet of aircraft is actually a fleet of multiple different kinds of cost-differentiated aircraft variants—requires additional information on multiple purchase and support costs and the distribution of variants, as well as the associated calculations to obtain a fleet-wide aggregate. Adding realism that accounts for discounted value based on purchase dates, for example, requires even more data gathering and identification of the aircraft or launchers that are slated to participate in the strike mission. Widening the boundaries of the analysis to, for example, include (1) the cost of the command and control system that allows for the sharing of targeting information, (2) the cost of securing fuel and munitions depots for both air and ground assets, or (3) the cost of transporting launchers and aircraft from the continental United States to theater requires collecting data on the associated cost elements in addition to the platforms actually used in the strike operation. An estimate that accounts for these elements is generally more realistic—meaning it comes closer to reflecting the cost of conducting strike in the real world—than one that does not.

Applying the Data

After the needed data elements have been collected, they must be combined to form a coherent cost estimate. As with finding the data, challenges related to applying the data likely grow with broader boundaries and greater detail. Costs that accrue from peripherals or activities that are farther removed from the effects that most immediately aim to achieve the objectives—the costs that would be included in an estimate with more detail or broader boundaries—can be harder to attribute to a given mission than others.

In our strike example, the procurement cost of equipment and munitions can be easily attributed to the strike mission because equipment and munitions are directly employed and even used up. O&S costs are somewhat more difficult to estimate and attribute, but for a single strike mission, such costs are likely to amount to much less than the cost of expended munitions and attrited equipment. O&S costs for ground-based platforms could be computed using Army cost estimate factors that escalate platform costs to account for the direct support cost components of O&S (parts and fuel) to reflect wartime demands along with some special pays for deployed soldiers. Army platform O&S cost inputs are based on an annual peacetime projection, thus requiring the wartime escalator to reflect the expectation that the unit will increase its OPTEMPO during war (it will drive more miles, burn more gas, require more spare parts, etc.). For aircraft, O&S cost factors are already expressed in terms of a discrete unit of activity: the flying hour. Therefore, at first order, they do not appear to require this type of wartime cost escalation as long as flying hours can be attributed to the mission. Although it could be defensible for a cost analyst to inflate ground-based O&S costs without inflating aircraft O&S costs, accepting this inconsistency is an example of the kind of judgment-based decisions that must be made to complete the analysis. Attempting to instead estimate the difference between peacetime and wartime cost-per-flying-hour—or the number of hours that would have been flown in either instance—would further increase the difficulty of the analysis, possibly without having a significant effect on the overall cost estimates.

More generally, to attribute O&S costs to a mission, an analyst must either know or make a judgment about how these costs relate to the mission. Furthermore, the analyst must choose to allocate all, some, or none of the costs to the mission. At the far end of the spectrum, a simple cost analysis could include all or none of the O&S costs that accrue during the mission, but it would be more realistic to include the marginal costs that the Army must bear over and above the costs of owning and operating a given platform, regardless of whether the Army goes to war (i.e., the costs it would already pay for unit training at a home station). The same goes for aircraft. However, splitting out the marginal O&S costs and doing so consistently across platforms can be very difficult. Additionally, a more realistic representation of the paths from technologies to the objective likely means the analyst must make a larger number of such decisions about cost allocation, further increasing the difficulty of the exercise.

Transferability of Economic Analysis Concepts to Other Applications

In this chapter, we have presented an application of CEA to a notional strike example and shown how some of the theoretical challenges captured in Chapter 3 could arise even in a setting with limited complexity and realism.

We can translate the theoretical framing to other technology applications. To do so would require, as it does in our strike application, defining the framing features and attributes of the problem space to include the alternative technologies, the objective, the effects, the costs, the ancillary benefits, the unintended consequences, and any sources of risk and uncertainty for the analysis. Computing, usefully applying CEA, and deriving a CPO metric to answer the question about the technology choice would then also require grappling with the set of analytic challenges, such as data availability and computational demand, laid out in this and the previous chapter. Table 4.2 highlights the needed framing features, specification requirements, and analytic challenges that might arise for each feature.

If an appropriate specification is possible and the analytic challenges can be overcome, the application of CEA and derivation of a CPO metric should be able to proceed much as it did for the strike example. However, even if the basic approach is the same, we might expect to see substantial differences across the applications not just in the specification of the technology or the objective but also in the cost estimation because the cost drivers and the relative order of magnitude of different cost components can be very different for applications outside strike. In the strike model, attrition and direct munitions expenditures are the major cost drivers, meaning that contextual risk related to attrition (Red attrition rates and OPTEMPO) and munition effectiveness (Blue p_ks) are of primary concern. In other applications, other cost factors—and thus other risks and uncertainties—might be more influential.

TABLE 4.2

Framing a Technology Choice as a Cost-Effectiveness Analysis

Framing Feature	Specification Requirement	Analytic Challenges
Technology description	• Sufficiently clear description of the technologies—meaning the potential means for achieving the objective through performing some activities	• Existence of flexible and/or joint technologies

Objective (fixed, measurable)	• A fixed and measurable objective or set of comparable objectives that enables the normalization of benefits across technology options
	• Examples of objectives unrelated to strike might include
	  – increasing survivability of ground forces in an area
	  – executing a wet gap crossing
	  – disrupting enemy lodgment.
		• Lack of a singular, fixed, and measurable objective or set of comparable objectives
		• Risk or uncertainty around the context in which the objective must be achieved

Effects	• Effects are the immediate consequences of activities undertaken by the technologies that might contribute to meeting the objective.
	• Examples of effects unrelated to strike might include
	  – disabling or destroying enemy multiple rocket launchers
	  – suppressing enemy fires in a crossing area
	  – employing shore-to-ship fires to strike enemy maritime forces.
		• Feasibility of modeling effects at the level or with the realism required for assessing whether the objective has been met and for computing cost estimates
		• Data availability for necessary effect-modeling parameters

Costs	• Value of expended resources (explicit and implicit), including
	  – direct costs of munitions or other expenditures
	  – attrition costs
	  – support and other indirect costs
	  – rent
		• Boundaries of the included cost elements
		• Data availability for the included cost elements

Ancillary benefits	• Positive results other than those directly related to the objective(s), meaning additional benefits of the technology that are not valued in the objective	• Existence of ancillary benefits • Lack of clarity on whether ancillary benefits should be considered as part of the objective or are decision-relevant • Data availability
Unintended consequences	• Negative results other than those directly related to the objective(s), such as drawbacks of the technology that do not prevent the technology from meeting the objective	• Existence of unintended consequences • Lack of clarity on whether unintended consequences should be considered as part of the objective or are decision-relevant • Data availability

CHAPTER 5

Moving Ahead with Economic Analysis and Metrics

In this report, we explored some of the potential strengths and limitations of CEA and related metrics. The intent of this work is to inform the Army and DoD communities about whether, when, and how to usefully employ CEA and related metrics, including the CPE and CPO. A 2020 policy paper from the Mitchell Institute, which proposed widespread use of an approach to economic analysis that would rely heavily on the derivation of a single CPE metric, has drawn attention to that metric in the defense community as an alternative to comparing the CPU of weapon systems (Deptula and Birkey, 2020). Knowing that one weapon system might cost some tens or hundreds of millions of dollars less than another from a CPU estimate provides little insight to its relative merit as an instrument of national security.

Findings on the Applicability of Cost-Effectiveness Analysis and Related Metrics

A comparison of the cost effectiveness of different technologies—as opposed to the CPU of different technologies—can, at least theoretically, account for some of the differences in the technologies' capabilities, support costs, and other less direct costs of technology employment. However, CEA and related metrics, such as the CPE or CPO, are not sufficient for capturing all the salient features or aspects of all problem spaces. CEA and related metrics, such as the CPE or CPO, can be more or less *feasible* and *useful* as tools to support decisionmaking depending on the circumstances.

In general, the less complex a problem or the less realistic the depiction of a problem, the easier it is to undertake an economic analysis, such as a CEA, and the more comprehensively a CPE, CPO, or other metric can summarize the information contained in the analysis. Assessing cost effectiveness and developing associated metrics is most *feasible* when a specific set of conditions either holds for the problem at hand or can be treated as if those conditions hold in a less realistic portrayal of the problem. The following conditions increase the feasibility of conducting a CEA and deriving related metrics:

- There is a single fixed and measurable objective—where fixed is defined as known, bounded, and unchanging—or a limited set of comparable objectives that are also fixed and measurable.
- There are relatively few (or minor) ancillary benefits and unintended consequences.
- The technologies being chosen from can operate independently.
- The context for achieving the objective is well understood by the decisionmaker and not highly variable.
- The boundaries of the problem space and cost elements lack ambiguity.
- The problem space and cost elements lack substantial risk or uncertainty.
- Sufficient data and computational capacity are available for conducting the analysis given the representation of the problem at hand.

Although these criteria might bear on all the forms of economic analysis that we introduced in Chapter 2, the first criterion, related to a single fixed and measurable objective, is especially important in a CEA because all the costs in a CEA must be assessed in relation to an objective. Thus, the further the problem veers from a single fixed and measurable objective, the more difficult the analysis becomes. This criterion is perhaps even more important for developing a CPO-type metric from the analysis because the objective is the denominator; that is, the distillation of the analysis to a point estimate that normalizes on the objective necessitates yet greater clarity than setting out the costs, ancillary benefits, unintended consequences, etc. because the objective anchors the calculation of the point estimate. A CBA might allow more leeway to consider broader circumstances—including comparisons across disparate objectives—and a BCA could be yet more expansive if it incorporates the findings from a CEA or CBA and supplements them by employing other analytical techniques. Of course, both a CBA and BCA could entail other challenges relating, for example, to additional analytical and data requirements, such as those for measurement and monetization.

Although feasibility is a prerequisite for usefulness, being able to conduct an economic analysis does not necessarily imply that using the results of the analysis will lead to good decisions. For a highly complex problem, it could be possible to construct a stylized analytic representation—in particular by relinquishing some realism—and use it to conduct to economic analysis and derive related metrics. However, as the analytic representation moves far enough away from the underlying problem, the application of economic analysis might no longer answer the desired question. Therefore, we add that **conducting an economic analysis and developing associated metrics is most *useful* when the models used to represent the pursuit of the objective can incorporate sufficient realism to encompass the salient features of the problem space**. Although saliency matters for all forms of economic analysis, the set of real-world problems that can be aptly translated into a CEA and captured in its metrics might be smaller than it is for a CBA or BCA because a CEA tends to be narrower.

Figure 5.1 provides a notional depiction of our interpretation of the feasibility and use-fulness of economic analysis, where *feasibility* refers to the technical ability to conduct an analysis or compute a related metric and *usefulness* refers to whether or to what extent the analysis and metrics can meaningfully inform the question at hand. Many modeling exercises are technically possible, but not all of them will add value to a decisionmaking process. In general, complications of the type discussed in Chapters 3 and 4 increase as one moves to the right—that is, from tactical to more strategic concerns, along the lines of the progression from an engagement to a campaign.

Using a single CPO metric to underpin an economic decision can lead to different decisions depending on assumptions about the context parameters and decisions about cost estimation. Excursions that explore the effect of objective definition, context, and decisions about bounding the analysis of effects and costs are required to build an understanding of the trade-offs among costs across technologies. **Making decisions based on a single metric can be risky, especially when the results of an economic analysis are highly sensitive to modeling decisions and assumptions, with the results of a CEA being additionally sensitive to the definition of the objective.** In the strike example provided in Chapter 4, many such excursions would be required to fully understand the problem space and explore the impact of the assumptions, presenting a significant need for modeling, costing, and assessment. This suggests that even this example of a simple strike mission could be approaching a level of complexity and realism where a cost-effectiveness metric ceases to be *useful,* in that it does not provide salient information for making decisions across enough of the problem space.

Finally, we reiterate that CEA and related metrics cannot speak to the question of whether achieving an objective is worth the cost of achieving it, by any means, even if the analysis can identify a definitive cost-minimizing technology. Rather, a CEA can, at best, speak to the preferability of one option over others. Thus, we might imagine that the threshold for the likely usefulness of a CEA might be somewhat lower than for a CBA or BCA, but, because they can present additional analytical and data requirements, a CBA or BCA might be less feasible than a CEA.

FIGURE 5.1

Feasibility and Usefulness of Economic Analysis

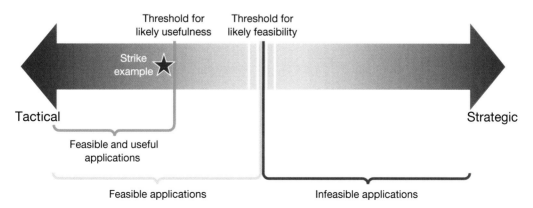

Recommendations

Neither CEA nor any other form of economic analysis can universally provide the information needed to make the best decision across all acquisition and operational questions. Rather, the analysis, including any metrics that derive from it, can provide valuable information and insights under certain circumstances, and these circumstances can differ somewhat depending on the method of analysis. The findings above offer guidance on the circumstances under which economic analysis generally and CEA more specifically can be both feasible and useful. Below, we provide recommendations for how analysts can use these findings to inform the development of future economic analyses.

- **Analysts should consider whether they can *feasibly* meet the specification, computational, and data requirements for the type of economic analysis that they intend to pursue.** In a choice between alternative technologies, the specification requirements would include the technology alternatives, the objectives, the effects, the costs, the ancillary benefits, the unintended consequences, and any sources of risk and uncertainty for the analysis. Specification requirements for an economic analysis of technology choice similar to our strike example are provided in Table 4.2.
- **Analysts should consider whether the *feasible* representation of the problem they have specified produces a *useful* economic analysis that can represent the salient features of the real-world problem.** Even if the specification, computational, and data requirements can be met, an economic analysis that does not adequately represent the problem space will fail to usefully inform decisionmaking. If the complexity of a real-world problem is too great, the realism with which it is feasible to represent the problem might not be enough to capture the salient features of the problem space.
- **Analysts should refrain from relying solely on CEA and related CPE or CPO metrics when (1) the real-world problem cannot be portrayed reasonably with either a single fixed and measurable objective or a limited set of comparable objectives, or (2) the real-world decision requires an assessment of net benefits.** Although concerns about the feasibility and usefulness of economic analysis should always be considered, these specific features of a decision problem should lead analysts to consider alternatives or complements to CEA.
- **Analysts should consider the risks of using a single metric (such as a CPE, CPO, or net benefit estimate) for decision support.** If varying the assumptions or the extent of realism within reasonable bounds would lead to changes in the decision that would be made based on the CPE, CPO, or net benefit estimate, then the metrics might not be suitable tools for making those decisions.

Future work on the cost effectiveness of ground-based long-range precision fires should consider these limitations when both devising and applying the results of economic analyses. Analysts should consider whether and how changes in assumptions or the extent of realism in an economic analysis affect the overall conclusions. For example, an economic analysis at the single engagement level might support different conclusions than one at the battlefield or campaign level. As illustrated in this report, different assumptions about platform capabilities, adversary tactics, and future operating environments—and the level of uncertainty around these assumptions—could lead to different decisions, as could different assumptions about what to include in the costs. For a complex question of military technology choice, it might also be wise to work with a broader type of economic analysis (such as a CBA or BCA) that can include disparate objectives and multiple metrics across a variety of assumptions and to complement quantitative assessments with more-qualitative information on the relative merits of the alternatives.

Glossary of Terms Related to Economic Analysis

The glossary in this appendix (Table A.1) covers the vocabulary that we use to discuss our framing of CPO in economic terms. It includes vocabulary that relates to how we set up our analyses, how we compare technology alternatives in those analyses, and the types of questions that we can answer with different forms of analysis.

TABLE A.1

Definitions of Economic and Related Terms

Term	Definition
Setting up the analysis	
Activity	Use of a resource, such as the use of a weapon system
Boundedness	Extent to which something (e.g., objective or cost) has clear, accepted limits
Context	Behavioral (e.g., strategic or nonstrategic) and nonbehavioral (e.g., physical, spatial, temporal, or other environmental) characteristics that define a particular situation or describe the state of the world
Effect	Immediate consequence of an activity, such as using a weapon system to destroy a target, that might contribute to meeting an objective
Fixity	Extent to which an objective is known, bounded, and unchanging
Flexible technology	Means that can produce or meet more than one effect or objective (this *or* that) but not simultaneously or within a given period or situation, such as an engagement
Joint technology	Means that can produce or meet more than one effect or objective (this *and* that) either simultaneously or within a given period or situation, such as an engagement
Objective	Statement of the intended result, such as the success of an engagement or mission, which might depend on obtaining particular effects
Risk	The potential for multiple outcomes that are knowable and for which likelihood is measurable (e.g., as a matter of probability and severity, in common military usage, or mean and variance, in economic analysis)[a]
Separable technology	Means that do not interact with any other means and, for our purposes, cannot produce or meet more than one effect or objective
Technology	Means, including combinations of activities (such as the use of several different weapon systems), of producing an effect or meeting an objective
Uncertainty	The potential for multiple outcomes that are either unknowable or, even if knowable, for which likelihood is not measurable

Table A.1—Continued

Comparing technology alternatives

Ancillary benefits | Positive results other than those of the objective(s)

Benefit | Value of gains from expending resources, which can be framed quantitatively or qualitatively (e.g., obtaining effects or meeting an objective)

Cost | Value of expended resources (explicit and implicit)

Net benefits | Benefits minus costs

Rent | A type of cost that can capture the value of allocated resources in alternative uses; it is an implicit rate based on the marginal value of next-best use

Spillovers | The combination of ancillary benefits and unintended consequences (i.e., additional good and bad results) that emerge from efforts to meet an objective but that are not part of that objective.

Unintended consequences | Negative results other than those of the objective(s)

Answering resource allocation questions

Admissibility | An alternative allocation of resources is worth it, generally implying that its benefits outweigh its costs (the net benefit is positive), ideally after accounting for all ancillary benefits, unintended consequences, risks, and uncertainties

Preferability | An alternative allocation of resources is better than others, generally implying that it either yields the most net benefit or entails the least cost

[a] Army Techniques Publication 5-19 defines risk as the "[p]robability and severity driven chance of loss, caused by threat or other hazards" (Headquarters, Department of the Army, *Risk Management*, Army Techniques Publication 5-19, November 9, 2021, p. Glossary-2), whereas other sources, especially those in the economics and finance literature, account for the possibility of both losses and gains by considering the expected value and potential downward and upward variability of the outcome. This literature uses the term *outcomes* broadly to cover a variety of possible results, consequences, or instances, including the selling price of a stock or whether a coin lands on heads or tails. For an example from the economics and finance literature, see Pindyck and Rubinfeld, 2018.

[b] See the fuller note on the distinction between risk and uncertainty in Chapter 3.

Depicting Cost-Effectiveness Analysis in Pictures

In this appendix, we depict CEA in a series of figures: first, with generic paths from technologies to objectives that do not name the technologies, effects, or objectives, and second, to a highly stylized strike mission that is similar to the notional example that we drew from in Chapter 4.

Drawing Cost Effectiveness with Generic Technology Paths

We start with a simple case, involving a single fixed and measurable objective, and then explore the implications of working in a problem space with greater complexity, stemming from ancillary benefits, unintended consequences, multiple objectives, flexible or joint technologies, and sequential or nested objectives. In each case, we compare different means of eliciting effects that can meet—or exceed—one or more objectives at different costs. We refer to the *means*, consisting of different combinations or sets of activities, as *technologies*. Although we do not probe the implications of risk or uncertainty, we point to circumstances in which they might affect the results of an analysis.

Figure B.1, which depicts our simple case, sets out three technologies—consisting of A_0, (A_1, A_2), and (A_3, A_4)—and the *paths*—through the effects E_0, E_1, and E_2—by which they can be used to meet one fixed and measurable objective, $O_{0,0}$. The three technologies and the paths that connect them to the objective are separable in that none of the paths has any bearing on any other. As the notation suggests, the effects (E_0, E_1, and E_2) need not be the same, but they must be sufficient to meet the objective. Stated slightly differently, the objective, itself, serves as a constraint on the choice of technology. We distinguish the objective by both type and level (0,0) to account for the possibility of different types of objectives occurring at different levels (e.g., battlefield or campaign) later in our analyses.

A comparative analysis could entail calculating, for each path to meeting or exceeding the objective, something like a CPE metric but instead oriented toward the objective as the cost-per-objective (i.e., a ratio of the cost of meeting or exceeding the objective by a particular path to a non-monetary measure of the objective). However, if we limit the analysis to cases of just meeting the objective (constraint)—or assume that any excess has no value and there

FIGURE B.1

Single Objective with Multiple Separable Technologies

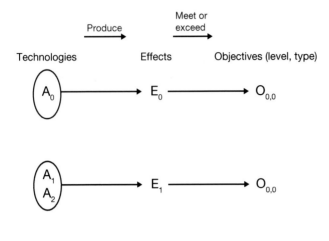

Different technologies, consisting of different combinations of activities (A's), yield effects (E's) that meet the same objective ($O_{0,0}$) separately. In this case, pick the least costly path—i.e., the minimum of the costs of A_0, (A_1,A_2), and (A_3,A_4), represented as $C(A_0)$, $C(A_1,A_2)$, and $C(A_3,A_4)$—to elicit E_0, E_1, or E_2 and obtain $O_{0,0}$.

are no ancillary benefits or unintended consequences—then, for all practical purposes, this will amount to a simple cost-minimization exercise, and the comparative metrics would just be the costs of eliciting the effects and meeting the objective by each path.[1]

In a departure from that simplicity, we can also consider the possibility that a technology meets a single objective but that the technology or its effects also generate spillovers: specifically, ancillary benefits or unintended consequences (Figure B.2).[2] In that case, we would need to decide how to factor in the spillovers. Arguably, these are equivalent to additional outputs—positive and negative, respectively—of the technologies or effects. Regardless of how we label the spillovers, they require assessment because they are not embodied in the stated objective. To value the spillovers, one would need to apply consistent designation rules. For example, ancillary benefits could be converted to objective-equivalent units or framed as cost offsets, but they must be treated the same way across analyses; otherwise, the calculations will be noncomparable.[3] In Figure B.2 and in each subsequent figure, we single out different sources of complexity incrementally with red, bold font.

---

[1] In this simple case, as depicted in Figure B.1, we would not need to distinguish between effects and objectives because eliciting the former would equate to obtaining the latter.

[2] If an objective yields specific ancillary benefits and unintended consequences, regardless of the technology or effects, then those benefits and consequences would not affect the comparison of paths.

[3] OMB (2003, p. 12) discusses some of the implications of ancillary benefits for conducting a CEA and how to address them:

FIGURE B.2

Single Objective with Multiple Separable Technologies and Spillovers

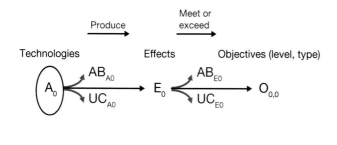

Different technologies, consisting of different combinations of activities (A's), elicit effects (E's) that meet the same objective ($O_{0,0}$) separately, but the A's and E's can entail different ancillary benefits (ABs) and unintended consequences (UCs). In this case, pick the least costly path, subject to any offsets for ABs or UCs.

If a technology were to produce an effect or effects that exceeded the objective, we could consider treating the excess as an ancillary benefit, but if we were not sure about the magnitude of the objective, we might want to represent the excess as excess. In that case, the excess could have value as a cushion against the possibility of a shortfall and be treated as presenting an *option* with which to meet emerging needs.[4]

Lastly, there could be some instances in which a result can be construed as either an ancillary benefit or an additional objective, depending on its importance to leadership. In this

When you can estimate the monetary value of *some* but not all of the ancillary benefits of a regulation, but [you] cannot assign a monetary value to the primary measure of effectiveness, you should subtract the monetary estimate of the ancillary benefits from the gross cost estimate to yield an estimated net cost. (This net cost estimate for the rule may turn out to be negative—that is, the monetized benefits exceed the cost of the rule.) If you are unable to estimate the value of some of the ancillary benefits, the cost-effectiveness ratio will be overstated, and this should be acknowledged in your analysis. CEA does not yield an unambiguous choice when there are benefits or costs that have not been incorporated in the net-cost estimates.

[4] In broad terms, "[a]n option offers the right, but not the obligation to take specific future actions depending on how uncertain future conditions evolve . . ." (Angelis, Ford, Dillard, 2015, p. 349). Like Angelis, Ford, and Dillard (2015), we are concerned in this report with *real options*, which involve tangible assets, as opposed to *financial options*, which involve financial instruments that typically convey a contractual right to buy or sell something under specific, predetermined conditions. Later in this and the next appendix, we discuss other cases in which we might think of a technology as creating an option-like opportunity and consequently presenting additional value in the decisionmaking process. For example, other ancillary-type benefits might be treated as options for obtaining alternative objectives.

case, the underlying reality does not change—the technology produces what it produces—but how we think about it changes. That is, the output might be seen as either an "extra" or a "necessity," depending on leadership's perspective. If, for example, a technology is fast enough to enable its use to both destroy the targets that must be destroyed to meet a stated objective and to eliminate another target that is valuable but—in leadership's eyes—nonessential, then we could frame the opportunity as an ancillary benefit; if instead leadership indicates that the target is essential, we could frame it as a second objective.

If there are multiple fixed objectives in a single level and both they and the underlying technologies are separable, then we can consider meeting each independently (Figure B.3); if a technology can contribute to more than one objective or if either the technologies or objectives are competing or complementary, then we might need to consider them together.

As depicted in Figure B.4, we can still choose among the technologies for meeting the objectives independently—that is, we can consider the best ways to meet $O_{0,0}$ without regard to meeting $O_{0,1}$, and vice versa—if the technologies can be used *flexibly* to meet **either** $O_{0,0}$ **or** $O_{0,1}$ (just one objective at a time). A technology, such as A_1A_2, might look like a bad choice for meeting one objective and a good choice for meeting another depending on the relative costs of the other feasible technologies for meeting each objective. Moreover, the flexibility to use a technology to meet either of the two objectives, as need arises, could hold value of its own (e.g., if there is any doubt about the necessity of meeting one objective or the other).[5] As the number of "or" statements increases between activities and effects or between effects and

FIGURE B.3

Multiple Objectives with Multiple Separable Technologies

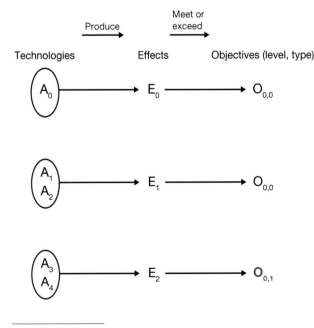

A_0 or (A_1,A_2), can be used to obtain $O_{0,0}$, separately, and (A_3,A_4) can be used to obtain $O_{0,1}$, separately (and must obtain *both* $O_{0,0}$ *and* $O_{0,1}$). In this case, treat the decisions for each objective independently—i.e., pick the minimum of $C(A_0)$ and $C(A_1,A_2)$ to obtain $O_{0,0}$, and incur $C(A_3,A_4)$ to obtain $O_{0,1}$.*

* If another technology were available to obtain $O_{0,1}$, then choose between that and (A_3,A_4) to obtain $O_{0,1}$, without regard to decisions about $O_{0,0}$.

---

[5] We discuss this possibility in greater detail in Appendix C.

FIGURE B.4

Multiple Objectives with Flexible Technologies

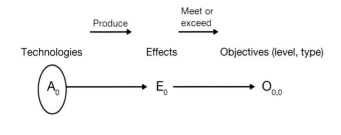

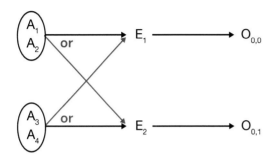

A_0 can be used to obtain $O_{0,0}$ and (A_1,A_2) and (A_3,A_4) can be used flexibly to obtain *either* $O_{0,0}$ or $O_{0,1}$ (and must obtain *both* $O_{0,0}$ *and* $O_{0,1}$). In this case, treat the decisions for each objective independently—i.e., pick the minimum of $C(A_0)$, $C(A_1,A_2)$, and $C(A_3,A_4)$ to obtain $O_{0,0}$, and the minimum of $C(A_1,A_2)$ and $C(A_3,A_4)$ to obtain $O_{0,1}$.

objectives, such flexibility—and its inherent benefits—would also increase, but the computational challenges of identifying the best path or combination of paths would grow too.

By contrast, if, as Figure B.5 depicts, the technology A_1,A_2 can meet both objectives simultaneously within a given period or in the same situation—what we refer to as a *joint technology*—we would need to consider the least-cost paths to obtaining the two objectives ($O_{0,0}$ **and** $O_{0,1}$) together.[6] That is, when any one of the technologies can meet both objectives at the same time, we must consider the objectives—and the various means of attaining them—collectively, as a package. As before, the ability to do more than one thing with a technology can also hold value of its own, especially in the face of risk or uncertainty, regarding needs.

If all the objectives, such as $O_{0,0}$ and $O_{0,1}$, were not equally important, then we would need to consider the relative merit of each objective, as with weights or a trading scheme, but that might challenge the notion of fixity, depending on whether the weights are stable or if some objectives drop from view.[7] If we were unsure about decisionmakers' preferences

---

[6] Hereafter, we write "simultaneously" for brevity, but we mean "simultaneously, within a given period, or in the same situation," such as an engagement. For simplicity, we also assume that simultaneity does not entail any additional cost; if it did, we would need to factor the costs into the analyses.

[7] For a concrete example of weighting, we recommend the simple problem presented in Angelis, Ford, and Dillard, 2015, pp. 352–354. For a broader overview of multiobjective decisionmaking that discusses different methods of comparison and aggregation, we suggest Kent D. Wall and Cameron A. MacKenzie, "Multiple Objective Decision Making," in Francois Melese, Anke Richter, and Binyam Solomon, eds., *Military Cost-Benefit Analysis: Theory and Practice,* Routledge, 2015.

FIGURE B.5
Multiple Objectives with a Joint Technology

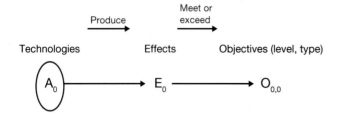
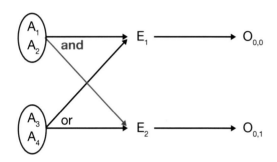

(A_1, A_2) can be used to obtain both $O_{0,0}$ *and* $O_{0,1}$ jointly, meaning simultaneously (and must obtain *both* $O_{0,0}$ and $O_{0,1}$). In this case, compare the costs of combinations of activities that result in both $O_{0,0}$ and $O_{0,1}$, together—i.e., pick the minimum of $C(A_1, A_2)$, $(C(A_0) + C(A_3, A_4))$, $2 \times C(A_3, A_4)$ to obtain both $O_{0,0}$ and $O_{0,1}$.

(e.g., because of imperfect information or shifting environmental conditions), we could seek to obtain the combination of technologies that would stand up to a broad variety of possible preferences and conditions.

Figure B.6 depicts a case in which both of the technologies (A_1, A_2 and A_3, A_4) that can meet $O_{0,0}$ can also meet $O_{0,1}$ simultaneously, thereby rendering the technology (A_0) that can meet only $O_{0,0}$ superfluous. More generally, if all the technologies that can meet $O_{0,1}$ can also meet $O_{0,0}$ simultaneously—i.e., with an "and" statement connecting them—then any technologies that can meet only $O_{0,0}$ will be superfluous, assuming both $O_{0,0}$ and $O_{0,1}$ are necessary.[8] However, recalling Figure B.5, if there were any other technologies that could meet only $O_{0,1}$, it would still be necessary to compare, on the one hand, the costs of all the possible combinations of those technologies and any technologies that could meet only $O_{0,0}$ (i.e., the pairings of any complementary technologies that, together, can meet both objectives simultaneously), with, on the other hand, the costs of the already-joint technologies, to identify the least-cost path. In effect, the combined, complementary technologies serve the same role as the already-joint technologies. The same would be true, as was the case in Figure B.5, if there were a technology that could meet $O_{0,0}$ **or** $O_{0,1}$ because it could be paired with itself or other single-purpose technologies to meet both objectives. In any case, the presence of the joint technologies requires consideration of meeting both objectives together, as a package.

---

[8] The reverse would also be true: That is, if all the technologies that can meet $O_{0,0}$ can also meet $O_{0,1}$ simultaneously, then a technology that can meet only $O_{0,1}$ would be superfluous.

FIGURE B.6

Multiple Objectives with Joint Technologies That Dominate a Single-Purpose Technology

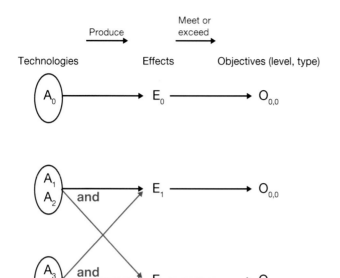

(A_1,A_2) and (A_3,A_4) can be used to obtain both $O_{0,0}$ *and* $O_{0,1}$ jointly, meaning simultaneously (and must obtain *both* $O_{0,0}$ *and* $O_{0,1}$). In this case, pick the minimum of $C(A_1,A_2)$ and $C(A_3,A_4)$. The first technology, A_0, is superfluous, because the chosen technology must obtain $O_{0,1}$ and other technologies obtain $O_{0,0}$ with $O_{0,1}$.

Identifying cost-minimizing solutions for variations on Figure B.6 with different "and" and "or" configurations can be easier or harder. For example,

- if A_1,A_2 and A_3,A_4 can achieve $O_{0,0}$ **and** $O_{0,1}$ (and **need only** obtain $O_{0,0}$ **or** $O_{0,1}$), pick the least costly of the three paths (this is like having only one objective).
- if A_1,A_2 and A_3,A_4 can achieve just $O_{0,0}$ **or** $O_{0,1}$ (and **need only** obtain $O_{0,0}$ **or** $O_{0,1}$), pick the least costly of the three paths (this is also like having only one objective).
- if A_1,A_2 and A_3,A_4 can achieve just $O_{0,0}$ **or** $O_{0,1}$ (and **must** obtain **both** $O_{0,0}$ **and** $O_{0,1}$), pick the minimum of $C(A_0)$, $C(A_1,A_2)$, and $C(A_3,A_4)$ to obtain $O_{0,0}$, and pick the minimum of $C(A_1,A_2)$ and $C(A_3,A_4)$ to obtain $O_{0,1}$, as shown in Figure B.4.

Alternatively, A_0 could be rendered superfluous if, as in Figure B.7, a combination of complementary effects is necessary to obtain an objective.

The position of the "and" statements in Figure B.7 does not indicate jointness, as defined previously, but rather indicates that success (obtaining $O_{0,1}$) requires eliciting both E_1 and E_2.

For multiple nested objectives, as might be the case in a campaign versus a battle, one could specify a set of objectives that would support another set of higher-level objectives, but one would also need to account for the possibilities of spillovers and other complexities. Figure B.8 shows, in a relatively simple case, how incorporating a second level of objectives— with some nesting—adds feasible paths and can introduce the possibility of seeking an effect, such as E_3, that might not have led directly to an immediate objective. Still, the solution set

FIGURE B.7
Multiple Objectives with Complementary Effects

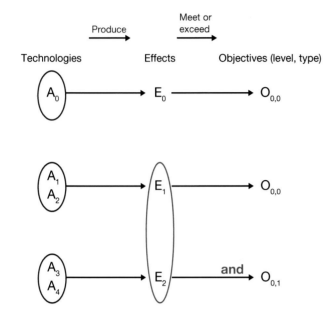

If both E_1 and E_2 are necessary to obtain $O_{0,1}$ (and *must* obtain *both* $O_{0,0}$ *and* $O_{0,1}$), then A_0 is superfluous, even if it is a less expensive path to $O_{0,0}$ than (A_1,A_2). In this case, undertake both (A_1,A_2) and (A_3,A_4) at a cost of $C(A_1,A_2) + C(A_3,A_4)$.

FIGURE B.8
Multiple Nested Objectives with Separable Technologies

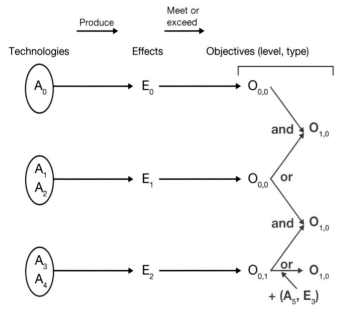

If only $O_{0,0}$ or $O_{0,1}$ is necessary at the initial level (0), different combinations of $O_{0,0}$ and/or $O_{0,1}$ can yield $O_{1,0}$ (higher-level objective), and an additional effect (E_3) can support $O_{1,0}$, then possible paths to $O_{1,0}$ consist of:

$2 \times O_{0,0}*$
$O_{0,0}* + O_{0,1}$
$O_{0,1}* + (A_5,E_3)$.

If $C(A_5)$ is sufficiently less than $C(A_0)$ and $C(A_1,A_2)$, then obtaining $O_{0,1}$ could be more desirable than obtaining $O_{0,0}$, even if cost of doing so is higher.

* By any means

shrinks quickly through pairwise comparisons. If you know where you need to go and can trace the paths to getting there, the decision reduces to a relatively simple cost-minimization problem, even with nested objectives. However, a key takeaway from this depiction is that nested goals tend to require forward-looking decisions. Arguably, much of the challenge of the analysis comes down to fixity, but longer paths can be harder to predict and, thus, might present challenges of their own.

As in Figure B.7, the position of the "and" statements in this figure does not indicate jointness but rather indicates that success requires accomplishing two things—that is, two occurrences of $O_{0,0}$ (by any means) or one occurrence **each of** $O_{0,0}$ **and** $O_{0,1}$—to obtain $O_{1,0}$.

Drawing Cost Effectiveness in a Highly Stylized Strike Mission

In this section, we shift from purely hypothetical depictions of activities, technologies, effects, objectives, and costs to a highly stylized representation of a strike mission. Specifically, we set out a weapon system allocation decision involving different combinations of two possible weapon systems (one air based and the other ground based) that can strike to achieve a fixed numerical objective (X) measured in terms of Red target kills. The use of each system is the *activity*, the combination of systems is the *technology*, the associated strikes are the *effect*, and the number of kills is the *objective*. By referring to combinations of the systems as *technologies*, we imply that different allocations of the systems constitute different technologies. Figure B.9 shows two bookend technologies that rely most and least heavily on air-based assets compared with ground-based assets (Technologies 1 and 2, respectively), as well as a representative interior technology (Technology 3).

Technology 1 relies solely on aircraft and meets the objective more slowly than a technology, such as Technology 2, that uses both aircraft and ground-based munitions, but the objective (X) is the same regardless of the technology. The speed of the mission, which is inherent to the technology choice, affects the accumulation of costs, unintended consequences, and ancillary benefits.[9] The technologies might yield different effects or entail different ancillary benefits or unintended consequences, but they will still meet the objective (i.e., Red target kills = X).

Technology 2 uses a mix of air- and ground-based assets, employing a maximum number of ground-based fires (maximum > 0) based on availability and then augmenting the ground-based fires with the fewest possible aircraft (aircraft = minimum > 0) to meet the objective. At least implicitly, we are assuming that a mixed-platform technology (aircraft and ground-based assets) can feasibly meet the objective. We do not solve for the optimal asset mix; instead, we assess the relative costs, ancillary benefits, and unintended consequences of the

---

[9] Alternatively, we could model time as a constraint and pick combinations of aircraft and ground-based fires that can meet the Red target kill objective within a specific amount of time at least cost subject to any other constraints or ancillary benefits and unintended consequences.

FIGURE B.9

Technology Alternatives and Associated Costs for a Strike Mission

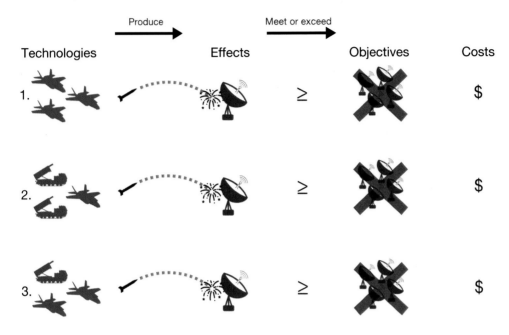

NOTE: Icons are intended to generally represent employment of a particular platform rather than provide specific counts. Aircraft icons represent air patrols, launcher icons represent ground-based launchers, red radar icons represent targets (with gray Xs representing the objective of destroying the targets), and munition icons represent needed munitions for this engagement. Technology 1 relies most heavily—indeed solely—on air-based assets, Technology 2 relies least heavily on air-based assets, and Technology 3 represents a middling case. The dollar symbols in the final column represent costs that differ by technology.

bookend technologies and a representative interior technology. In theory, we could find the optimal mix by assessing the costs, benefits, and attributes of all the feasible technologies—including the bookends and everything in between—and selecting the cost-minimizing technology among them.[10] In Table B.1, we summarize

- the attributes of the bookend technologies (Technologies 1 and 2) and third representative interior technology (Technology 3)
- the intended objectives and effects (which are the same for each technology)
- the potential costs, ancillary benefits, and unintended consequences (which could differ for each technology).

Insomuch as some of those differences are inherent to the technologies, we have sketched them out in the relevant table cell entries, even if we cannot quantify them without further

---

[10] The optimal solution could be a bookend solution—(aircraft > minimum, ground-based fires = 0) or (aircraft = minimum, ground-based fires = maximum)—or an interior solution (aircraft > minimum, ground-based fires < maximum).

TABLE B.1

Strike Technology Alternatives in the Language of Cost-Effectiveness Analysis

Attribute	Technology 1	Technology 2	Technology 3
Description	• Single platform (*Air Only*) • Aircraft > minimum; ground-based fires = 0 • Slower	• Mixed platform (ground max) • Aircraft = minimum; ground-based fires = maximum • Faster	• Mixed platform (middling case) • Aircraft > minimum, ground-based fires < maximum • Intermediate
Objective (fixed, measurable)	• Red target kills = X	• Red target kills = X	• Red target kills = X
Effects	• Strikes $\geq$ X[a]	• Strikes $\geq$ X	• Strikes $\geq$ X
Costs	• Execution (e.g., munitions) • Attrition (aircraft, ground-based fires) • Rent[b]	• Execution (e.g., munitions) • Attrition (aircraft, ground-based fires) • Rent	• Execution (e.g., munitions) • Attrition (aircraft, ground-based fires) • Rent
Ancillary benefits	• Less Blue ground attrition = 0 • Time savings = 0 • Unique activity option = 0	• Less Blue ground attrition $\geq$ 0 • Time savings $\geq$ 0 • Unique activity option $\geq$ 0	• Less Blue ground attrition $\geq$ 0 • Time savings $\geq$ 0 • Unique activity option $\geq$ 0
Unintended consequences	• More Blue other attrition • Casualties	• More Blue other attrition • Casualties	• More Blue other attrition • Casualties

NOTE: The values for the number of Red target kills and the threshold for strikes (i.e., X) would be the same for all three technology alternatives, but the values for the terms in the remaining rows—such as the amount of execution costs, the extent of attrition, the time savings—could differ.

[a] We assume that it is not possible to "kill" x Red targets with fewer than x strikes.

[b] *Rent* is an implicit rate based on marginal value of next best use other than in the strike mission.

analysis. A table such as this could be used to collate information pertaining to a CEA and, possibly, the results of a CEA.

Using Table B.1, we can reinterpret the figures from the previous section as depictions of Technologies 1, 2, and 3 to draw further insight. In Figures B.10 and B.11, we provide more-detailed depictions of the paths from activities to the objective (X) for each allocation, first without spillovers and then with spillovers.

Although not depicted in Figures B.10 or B.11, it is possible that one or more of the underlying weapon systems—hence technologies—can also meet an additional objective, perhaps uniquely. That is, ground-based assets might be able to accomplish something valuable that air-based assets cannot (or vice versa). If there is doubt about the relevance of the additional objective, we might treat the ground- or air-based asset's potential to meet the objective as having or creating an option value (see Appendix C). Figures B.3 through B.7, in which at least one of the three technologies can be used to obtain a second objective ($O_{0,1}$), set the stage for such possibilities.

FIGURE B.10

Depiction of the Weapon System Allocation Decision Without Spillovers

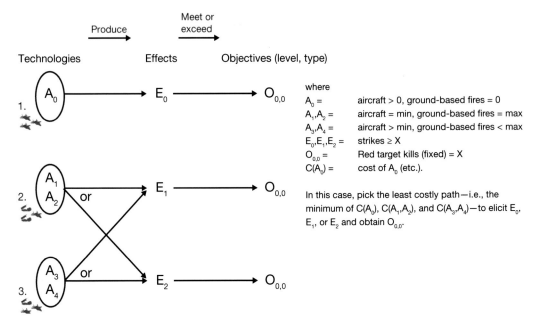

FIGURE B.11

Depiction of the Weapon System Allocation Decision with Spillovers

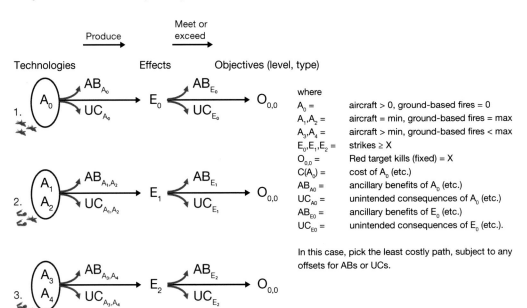

Here, we elaborate on the conditions depicted in Figures B.4 and B.5 to consider two cases in which ground-based assets can serve a unique role that enables the attainment of a second objective ($O_{0,1}$) that is unattainable with air power alone.[11]

Figure B.12 builds on Figure B.4 to depict a case in which Technologies 2 and 3 can afford enough ground power to obtain either the first or second objective ($O_{0,0}$ or $O_{0,1}$) but not to obtain both objectives simultaneously. In this case, as was true previously, if the need for the second objective ($O_{0,1}$) is unclear, then the technologies (A_1,A_2 and A_3,A_4) that can meet that objective might hold additional value because they preserve the option to meet it.

Figure B.13 builds on Figure B.5 to depict the case in which Technology 2 can be used to achieve both objectives simultaneously ($O_{0,0}$ and $O_{0,1}$), but Technology 3, which affords less ground power, can meet only one objective or the other ($O_{0,0}$ or $O_{0,1}$). In this case, as was true previously, the presence of a joint technology requires a joint decision about the two objectives. The potential for the dual-purpose technologies to hold value under conditions of doubt, such as those regarding the need for the second objective ($O_{0,1}$), also holds.

We can apply many of the insights from the prior figures to this analysis. Recalling Figure B.6, if both Technologies 2 and 3 can afford enough ground power to obtain the two objectives ($O_{0,0}$ and $O_{0,1}$) simultaneously, then Technology 1 will be superfluous. Generally, if one set of technologies can accomplish two things at once—or even separately—and another

FIGURE B.12

Depiction of the Weapon System Allocation Decision with Flexible Technologies and a Unique Role for Ground Power to Obtain a Second Objective

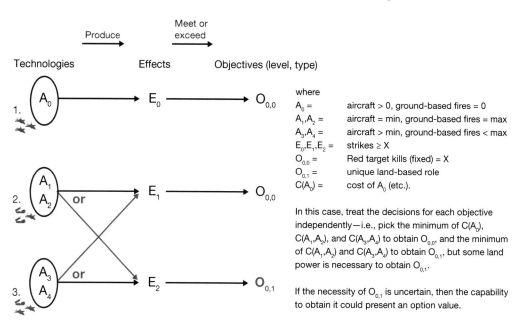

where
A_0 = aircraft > 0, ground-based fires = 0
A_1,A_2 = aircraft = min, ground-based fires = max
A_3,A_4 = aircraft > min, ground-based fires < max
E_0,E_1,E_2 = strikes ≥ X
$O_{0,0}$ = Red target kills (fixed) = X
$O_{0,1}$ = unique land-based role
$C(A_0)$ = cost of A_0 (etc.).

In this case, treat the decisions for each objective independently—i.e., pick the minimum of $C(A_0)$, $C(A_1,A_2)$, and $C(A_3,A_4)$ to obtain $O_{0,0}$, and the minimum of $C(A_1,A_2)$ and $C(A_3,A_4)$ to obtain $O_{0,1}$, but some land power is necessary to obtain $O_{0,1}$.

If the necessity of $O_{0,1}$ is uncertain, then the capability to obtain it could present an option value.

[11] The reverse case, when a second objective requires air power, could also hold.

FIGURE B.13

Depiction of the Weapon System Allocation Decision with a Joint Technology and a Unique Role for Ground Power to Obtain a Second Objective

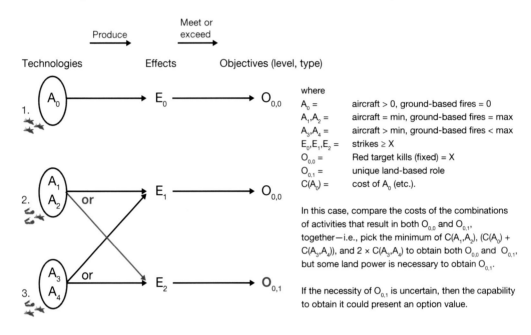

where
$A_0 =$ aircraft > 0, ground-based fires = 0
$A_1, A_2 =$ aircraft = min, ground-based fires = max
$A_3, A_4 =$ aircraft > min, ground-based fires < max
$E_0, E_1, E_2 =$ strikes ≥ X
$O_{0,0} =$ Red target kills (fixed) = X
$O_{0,1} =$ unique land-based role
$C(A_0) =$ cost of A_0 (etc.).

In this case, compare the costs of the combinations of activities that result in both $O_{0,0}$ and $O_{0,1}$, together—i.e., pick the minimum of $C(A_1,A_2)$, $(C(A_0) + C(A_3,A_4))$, and 2 × $C(A_3,A_4)$ to obtain both $O_{0,0}$ and $O_{0,1}$, but some land power is necessary to obtain $O_{0,1}$.

If the necessity of $O_{0,1}$ is uncertain, then the capability to obtain it could present an option value.

can accomplish only one, the technologies that can accomplish two things might be preferred because they dominate other technologies, impart flexibility to address current needs, or—with that flexibility—preserve the option to address unclear future needs. That said, it is also possible that air power can yield opportunities that ground power cannot and that, without sufficient air power—as might emerge, perhaps, from Technology 1 (but not Technologies 2 or 3)—those opportunities would be unattainable.

Lastly, as shown in Figure B.14, nested objectives could, as they did previously, require forward-looking thinking. For closer correspondence with our three-technology narrative, the terms of engagement in Figure B.14 differ slightly from those in Figure B.7; specifically, Technologies 2 and 3 (i.e., A_1, A_2 and A_3, A_4) can yield either of the initial objectives (i.e., $O_{0,0}$ or $O_{0,1}$). Given the inclusion of the two "or" statements, we can apply the term "by any means" to more paths than we could in our earlier rendering—that is, to include the paths that lead to and through $O_{0,1}$—which implies somewhat greater flexibility and might bear on costs.

FIGURE B.14

Depiction of the Weapon System Allocation Decision with Flexible Technologies, a Unique Role for Ground Power, and Nested Objectives

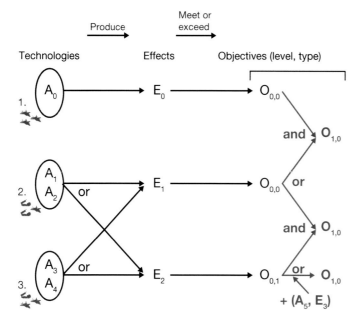

If only $O_{0,0}$ or $O_{0,1}$ is necessary at the initial level (0), different combinations of $O_{0,0}$ and/or $O_{0,1}$ can yield $O_{1,0}$ (higher-level objective), and an additional effect (E_3) can support $O_{1,0}$, then possible paths to O1,0 consist of:

$2 \times O_{0,0}^{*}$)
$O_{0,0}^{*} + O_{0,1}^{*}$
$O_{0,1}^{*} + (A_5, E_3)$.

If $C(A_5)$ is sufficiently less than $C(A_0)$ and $C(A_1, A_2)$, then obtaining $O_{0,1}$ could be more desirable than obtaining $O_{0,0}$, even if the cost of doing so is higher.

* By any means

Framing Flexibility as an Option Value

Much of the discussion in Appendix B assumes a *deterministic* environment; that is, activities (*A*'s) produce effects (*E*'s) with a probability of 1.0, and in turn, those effects contribute to the objectives (*O*'s) in a fully known, nonrandom manner. However, in many—if not most—real-world cases, the operating environment is subject to a great deal of risk and uncertainty, meaning that a priori (i.e., before events occur) effects produced by activities, the success in meeting objectives, and even some of the objectives are, at best, described with probability distributions.

In some cases, we might be able to adapt the definition of success to reflect these conditions; for example, a probabilistic view of success might be achieving a specific objective ($O_{0,0}$) with a probability of 0.9. Operationalizing this concept for moderate levels of complexity would likely require simulation models that are parameterized with the probability distributions of the relevant risk factors and random states of the world (e.g., p_ks, Blue and Red behaviors, etc.), thus producing random effects from activities that are then mapped into the overall probability of meeting an objective.

In other cases, we might instead consider the odds of needing to undertake activities to meet one objective or another in one way or another under different, as-yet-unknown conditions. Economists refer to this as a problem of *information* because decisionmakers must decide how to allocate resources (e.g., different types of weapon systems to a mission) but do not yet know what the future holds regarding the objective, let alone what resources they will need. In the discussion that follows, we consider how to frame this approach in terms of the option value of flexibility and incorporate it into an economic analysis.

Although a simulation strategy can incorporate many of the unknowns in the environment (e.g., by parameterizing the distributions of the random variables and modeling how Blue and Red players might react), traditional CEA and CBA does not incorporate the value of the ability to change course in response to changing information (in other words, the value of operational flexibility as at least some unknowns resolve over time).[1] Put another way, there might be some value in being able to make a decision at some point in the future (when

---

[1] For a related discussion and an example that applies real options to an acquisition decision, see Angelis, Ford, and Dillard, 2015, p. 349. This concept is different from the definition of a flexible technology, which can be used to produce different effects.

the available information is different) as opposed to making a decision today. The value of the ability to defer decisions is termed *option value*.[2]

We can apply the concept of option value and how it relates to more traditional cost analysis to the choice of using different technologies to create effects and satisfy objectives (thus obtaining the value added from the technologies).[3] Consider the following example.

Assume a choice between the use of Technology 1 (T1) and Technology 2 (T2) to achieve a strike mission over a two-day planning horizon. T1 includes just aircraft, while T2 includes all the aircraft contained in T1 plus ground-based fires. The cost of the use of each technology involves both fixed costs (FCt for technology t), and variable costs (VCt) per day of use. At the beginning of the planning period, the results from the use of each technology are deterministic for the first day, but two states (S1 and S2) are possible on the second day with probabilities p and $1 - p$, respectively. The second state (S2) always conveys a unique targeting opportunity for T2, but the first state (S1) never conveys this opportunity. Thus, the probability of facing S2 (hence, encountering the unique opportunity in the second period) is $1 - p$, and the probability of facing S1 (hence, not encountering the unique opportunity in the second period) is p. We assume that if the opportunity arises, there is a benefit (measured by a cost offset) of B.[4] Between day 1 and day 2, the state for day 2—either S1 or S2—becomes known. It is assumed that the length of time to achieve the strike mission is two days regardless of the state or the technology chosen.

This setup is similar to a choice between A_0 and (A_1, A_2) in Figure B.14. The strike mission is objective $O_{0,0}$, and the unique targeting opportunity is objective $O_{0,1}$. Because of the two states in period 2, the necessity of $O_{0,1}$ is not known because the opportunity to strike the unique target is not guaranteed.

We make the following assumptions about the costs, benefits, and probabilities of this problem:[5]

- $FC_1 = 800$ (aircraft)
- $FC_2 = FC_1 + 200 = 1,000$ (aircraft + ground-based fires)
- $VC_1 = 600$
- $VC_2 = VC_1 + 700 = 1,300$ (aircraft + ground-based fires)
- $B = 1,200$ (assumed to directly offset costs when T2 is used in S2)

---

[2] More specifically, *quasi-option value* is the gain in value from the deferred decision conditional on not making a decision now, whereas the *real option value* is the value of exercising a flexible decision regarding tangible assets. See Caleb Maresca, "Option Value, an Introductory Guide," Effective Altruism Forum, February 21, 2020; and Christian P. Traeger, "On Option Values in Environmental and Resource Economics," *Resource and Energy Economics*, Vol. 37, No. 1, August 2014.

[3] This example focuses on the real option value.

[4] Conceptually, this could also be interpreted as the opportunity for freed-up aircraft to strike additional targets in S2.

[5] The numbers in this example were designed to create an example with the desired properties; there is no guarantee of a positive option value.

Finally, we assume that decisionmakers are looking to minimize the costs of fulfilling the strike mission (including the possible unique targeting opportunity offset).[6]

Assuming no discounting over the two-day period and $p = 0.5$, a CEA in which T1 or T2 is chosen for the strike mission at the beginning of the planning period results in the selection of T1 for this parameterization. To demonstrate the result for this case, note that the expected net present values (NPVs) of the cost for each technology are as follows:

$$\text{NPV}_{T1}: FC_1 + p2VC_1 + (1 - p)2VC_1 = 800 + 0.5(2 \times 600) + 0.5(2 \times 600) = 2000$$

$$\text{NPV}_{T2}: FC_2 + p2VC_2 + (1 - p)(2VC_2 - B) = 1000 + 0.5(2 \times 1300) + 0.5(2 \times 1300 - 1200) = 3000.$$

Given that the expected NPV of costs are lower for T1, the optimal cost-minimizing choice when only one technology can be chosen is T1.[7]

The CEA above assumes an all-or-nothing decision on technology prior to the first day of operations. However, the use of T2, which includes ground-based fires, creates additional value because it allows us to leverage new information about the actual state in day 2 that emerges between days 1 and 2. To illustrate, note that the decisionmaker chooses the optimal technology conditional on the state of the world in each period and then forms expectations about the next period. Given the parameterization here, the cost-minimizing choice is to use T1 in the first period, T1 in the second period in S1, and T2 in the second period in S2:[8]

$$\text{Minimum costs day 1: } \min(FC_1 + VC_1, FC_2 + VC_2) = \min(800 + 600, 1000 + 1300) =$$
$$\min(1400, 2300) = 1400$$

$$\text{Minimum costs day 2, S1: } \min(VC_1, FC_2 - FC_1 + VC_2) = \min(600, 1000 - 800 + 1300) =$$
$$\min(600, 1500) = 600[9]$$

$$\text{Minimum costs day 2, S2: } \min(VC_1, FC_2 - FC_1 + VC_2 - B) = \min(600, 1000 - 800 + 1300 -$$
$$1200) = \min(600, 300) = 300.$$

---

[6] Although this simple example is constructed in a cost-minimization framework to complement the material in the rest of the report, more traditional real options analysis is done in a benefit-cost framework.

[7] This conclusion remains the same even if fixed costs for both technologies equal zero.

[8] We can rule out selecting T2 in the first period because of the underlying cost difference between T1 and T2 and the lack of any possible offsetting benefit from T2 in that period.

[9] Without loss of generality, we assume that only the difference in fixed costs between T1 and T2 accrues when T1 is used in the first period and T2 in the second.

Forming expectations over these optimal choices results in the following expression for costs associated with flexible decisionmaking:

$$NPV_{flex}: FC_1 + VC_1 + p(VC_1) + (1-p)(FC_2 - FC_1 + VC_2 - B) = 1400 + 0.5(600) + 0.5(300) = 1850.$$

Thus, the ability to deploy ground-based fires in the second period (but not the first) is valuable and worth an amount equal to the difference in expected costs $(2{,}000 - 1{,}850 = 150)$ to the Army over the course of this two-day campaign.[10] Technically, the 150 is a real option value (i.e., the willingness to pay to use the flexible technology to achieve multiple objectives) and, as such, helps answer the question of the *value* of a more expensive but flexible technology used in the strike mission.[11] In this case, because the technologies are *additive* in the sense that ground-based fires are an additional asset used as part of T2, the real option value can be interpreted as the return on adding ground-based fires to an air-based strike operation.

Although obviously a gross simplification of real-world examples, the main principle of real option analysis—specifically, evaluating the expected value of the optimal decision in each realized state of the world rather than the expected performance of a decision made prior to obtaining missing information about the state of the world—provides a means of incorporating the value of flexibility into analysis when conditions in the future lack certainty (as they often do) and of helping estimate the returns to related systems.

---

[10] The value is equal to the costs of choosing the minimum expected cost technology for both periods (T1) less the expected costs of the flexible solution.

[11] With this parameterization, the option value is decreasing in FC_1, FC_2, VC_2, and p and increasing in VC_1 and B.

Abbreviations

BCA	business case analysis
CBA	cost-benefit analysis
CEA	cost-effectiveness analysis
CPE	cost-per-effect
CPO	cost-per-objective
CPU	cost-per-unit
DoD	U.S. Department of Defense
DoDI	Department of Defense Instruction
ISR	intelligence, surveillance, and reconnaissance
JCIDS	Joint Capabilities Integration and Development System
O&S	operations and sustainment
OMB	Office of Management and Budget
OPTEMPO	operational tempo
p_k	probability of kill
ROI	return on investment

References

Angelis, Diana I., David Ford, and John Dillard, "Real Options in Military Acquisition: A Retrospective Case Study of the Javelin Anti-Tank Missile System," in Francois Melese, Anke Richter, and Binyam Solomom, eds., *Military Cost-Benefit Analysis: Theory and Practice*, Routledge, 2015.

Army Financial Management and Comptroller, "FORCES Information," webpage, Office of the Assistant Secretary of the Army, undated. As of July 5, 2023: https://www.asafm.army.mil/Cost-Materials/Cost-Models/#forces

Best, Katharina Ley, Victoria A. Greenfield, Craig A. Bond, Nathaniel Edenfield, Mark Hvizda, John C. Jackson, Duncan Long, Jordan Willcox, *Beyond Cost-per-Shot: Illustrating the Use of Economic Analysis and Metrics in Defense Decisionmaking*, 2023, Not available to the general public

Brealey, Richard A., and Stewart C. Myers, *Principles of Corporate Finance*, 6th ed., McGraw-Hill, 2000.

Business Case Website, homepage, undated. As of June 26, 2023: https://www.business-case-analysis.com

Camm, Frank, John Matsumura, Lauren A. Mayer, and Kyle Siler-Evans, *A New Methodology for Conducting Product Support Business Case Analysis (BCA): With Illustrations from the F-22 Product Support BCA*, RAND Corporation, RR-1664-AF, 2017. As of June 21, 2023: https://www.rand.org/pubs/research_reports/RR1664.html

Deptula, David A., and Douglas A. Birkey, *Resolving America's Defense Strategy-Resource Mismatch: The Case for Cost-per-Effect Analysis*, Mitchell Institute for Aerospace Studies, July 2020. As of August 24, 2023: https://mitchellaerospacepower.org/wp-content/uploads/2021/01/a2dd91_9eb547d3420d47bc932c95f7e949d024-1.pdf

DoD—*See* U.S. Department of Defense.

Enthoven, Alain, "How Systems Analysis, Cost-Effectiveness Analysis, or Benefit-Cost Analysis First Became Influential in Federal Government Program Decision-Making," *Journal of Benefit Cost Analysis*, Vol. 10, No. 2, Summer 2019.

GAO—*See* U.S. Government Accountability Office.

Greenfield, Victoria A., and Letizia Paoli, *Assessing the Harms of Crime: A New Framework for Criminal Policy*, Oxford University Press, 2022.

Headquarters, Department of the Army, *Economic Analysis: Description and Methods*, Department of the Army Pamphlet 415–3, September 28, 2018.

Headquarters, Department of the Army, *Risk Management*, Army Techniques Publication 5-19, November 9, 2021.

Knight, Frank, *Risk, Uncertainty, and Profit*, Houghton Mifflin Company, 1921.

Maresca, Caleb, "Option Value, an Introductory Guide," Effective Altruism Forum, February 21, 2020.

Melese, Francois, Anke Richter, and Binyam Solomon, "Introduction: Military Cost-Benefit Analysis," in Francois Melese, Anke Richter, and Binyam Solomon, eds., *Military Cost-Benefit Analysis: Theory and Practice*, Routledge, 2015.

Office of Management and Budget, *Regulatory Analysis*, Circular A-4, September 17, 2003.

Office of the Assistant Secretary of Defense for Logistics and Materiel Readiness, *DoD Product Support Business Case Analysis Guidebook*, U.S. Department of Defense, 2014.

OMB—*See* Office of Management and Budget.

Pindyck, Robert S., and Daniel L. Rubinfeld, *Microeconomics*, 9th ed., Pearson, 2018.

Public Law 116-283, William M. (Mac) Thornberry National Defense Authorization Act for Fiscal Year 2021; Section 147, Study on Measures to Assess Cost-per-Effect for Key Mission Areas, January 1, 2021.

Quade, E. S., "A History of Cost-Effectiveness," RAND Corporation, P-4557, 1971. As of June 21, 2023:
https://www.rand.org/pubs/papers/P4557.html

Rosen, Harvey S., *Public Finance*, 6th ed., McGraw-Hill, 2001.

Schmidt, Marty J., *The Business Case Guide*, 2nd ed., Solution Matrix, 2002.

Sheen, Raymond, and Amy Gallo, *HBR Guide to Building Your Business Case*, Harvard Business Review, July 7, 2015.

Traeger, Christian P., "On Option Values in Environmental and Resource Economics," *Resource and Energy Economics*, Vol. 37, No. 1, August 2014.

U.S. Department of Defense, *Economic Analysis for Decision-Making*, Department of Defense Instruction 7041.03, September 9, 2015, incorporating change 1, October 2, 2017.

Wall, Kent D., and Cameron A. MacKenzie, "Multiple Objective Decision Making," in Francois Melese, Anke Richter, and Binyam Solomon, eds., *Military Cost-Benefit Analysis: Theory and Practice*, Routledge, 2015.